THE HOLOCAUST
AND LIFE UNDER
NAZI OCCUPATION

Peter Darman, Editor

ROSEN PUBLISHING®

New York

This edition is published in 2013 by:

The Rosen Publishing Group, Inc.
29 East 21st Street, New York, NY 10010

For Brown Bear Books Ltd:
Editorial Director: Lindsey Lowe
Senior Editor: Tim Cooke
Military Editor: Peter Darman
Children's Publisher: Anne O'Daly
Art Director: Jeni Child
Picture Manager: Sophie Mortimer

Library of Congress Cataloging-in-Publication Data

The Holocaust and life under Nazi occupation/Peter Darman.—First.
    pages ; cm.—(World War II)
Includes bibliographical references and index.
ISBN 978-1-4488-9235-8 (library binding)
1. Holocaust, Jewish (1939–1945—Juvenile literature. 2. Jews—Persecutions—Germany—Juvenile literature.
3. World War, 1939–1945—Jews—Juvenile literature. 4. Germany—History—1933–1945—Juvenile literature. 5.
Germany—Ethnic relations—Juvenile literature. I. Darman, Peter, editor.
D804.34.H646 2013
940.53'18—dc23

2012030576

Manufactured in the United States of America

CPSIA Compliance Information: Batch #W13YA: For further information, contact Rosen Publishing, New York, at 1-800-237-9932

CONTENTS

CHAPTER 1
THE TERROR BEGINS

In their quest to establish a National Socialist state, the Nazis used the law and police to crush all forms of opposition. The result was a police state in which arbitrary arrests and state brutality ensured that all opposition was crushed. The first targets of the Nazis were the Jews and Communists.

Die Katze lässt das Mausen nia...

Die führende englische Zeitung „Daily Mail" berichtet:

„Die Beteiligung der Juden an Verbrechen gegen die englischen Kriegswirtschaftsgesetze hat das Judentum und den jüdischen Namen in England verfemt, erklärte der Großrabbiner Dr. J. Hertz in einer Londoner Synagoge."

Der Rabbi wollte mit diesen Vorhaltungen sicherlich seine Rassegenossen zur größeren Vorsicht bei ihren dunklen Schieberei ermahnen, damit das englische Volk nicht erkennt, welche Läuse es sich da in den Pelz gesetzt hat. Seine Bemühungen dürften jedoch vergeblich sein. So sind die Juden. Erst hetzen sie die Völker in den Krieg, und während die Soldaten dieser Völker kämpfen und bluten,

machen sie aus dem Kriege Geschäft, schachern, schieben und betrügen und füllen sich ihre schmutzigen Taschen auf Kosten ihrer Gastvölker. In Deutschland wurde ihnen das Handwerk gelegt. Wir haben sie von der deutschen Volksgemeinschaft abgesondert und sie mit dem gelben Judenstern gekennzeichnet. Jedermann weiß:

Wer dieses Zeichen trägt, ist ein Feind unseres Volkes

Jude

"Whoever wears this symbol is an enemy of our people." An anti-Semitic poster in pre-war Germany.

Once in power, Hitler was ruthless with all those who opposed him, even former comrades. One of the Nazis' most dramatic coups on coming to power was a purge of fellow Nazis considered a threat to the new regime. This perceived threat centered on Ernst Röhm, a hard, stocky man who had been a close friend of Hitler since the early 1920s. Röhm had been wounded three times in World

War I and bore the scars: half his nose was missing and his cheek was rutted by a bullet wound. Röhm had established the *Sturmabteilung* (Storm troopers or SA) in the 1920s to fight for the Nazis. It was Röhm's brown-shirted SA who won the street battles with the Communists, and Hitler was grateful to Röhm for his help prior to 1933. He proclaimed that he wanted "to thank Heaven for having given me the right to call a man like you my friend and comrade-in-arms."

However, once in power Hitler increasingly found Röhm an embarrassment and an alternative center of power. Röhm, along with other Nazis such as Gregor Strasser, formed a "left-wing" branch of Nazism. They stressed the "socialism" side to the National Socialist German Workers' Party, and called for a second workers' revolution; for Röhm, the Nazi movement was a working-class movement and revolution was a permanent state. Hitler, on the other hand, had come to power in 1933 with the help of Germany's reactionary élite of businessmen, politicians, and army officers.

Previous pages:
Child survivors of the Auschwitz death camp after their liberation by Soviet troops in January 1945.

HITLER'S BELIEFS

Anti-Semitism, or hatred of the Jews, was at the very core of Nazi beliefs. Hitler had made his hatred of the Jews clear as early as 1924. In that year he had written *Mein Kampf* (My Struggle). The book was a mixture of an autobiography and a collection of Hitler's beliefs. In the book Hitler blamed the Jews for Germany's defeat in World War I. He also blamed them for the economic hardship that followed the war. He said that Germany was at the mercy of an international Jewish conspiracy. Hitler's beliefs struck a chord with many Germans. Anti-Semitism had a long history in parts of central and

eastern Europe. The Jews had often been accused of trying to destroy Christian society. They were also caricatured for their traditional role in banking and moneylending. They were stereotyped as exploiting people in order to make money.

In Hitler's view, the Jews were the eternal enemies of the pure "Aryan" or "Germanic" people of northern Europe. It was the Nazis' aim to create an Aryan "super race." In order to achieve this, they would have to eliminate everyone of "inferior" race from the German heartland. Under the Nazis, schools taught hatred of Jews and Slavs and the superiority of the Aryan race.

The German armed forces and senior industrialists who had helped Hitler to power viewed Röhm with anxiety. Hitler knew that he had to assuage his new backers. The German armed forces suspected Röhm of having greater ambitions. One professional officer recalled how his comrades disliked the upstart SA: "One rejected the Storm troopers because of their behavior, the way they looked, the way they were … they were hated by most soldiers." Hitler tried to talk Röhm into his way of thinking. On June 4, 1934, he spent five hours with Röhm in an attempt to curb his wish for continued revolution. After several of these fruitless meetings, Hitler concluded that only force would

work. In June 1934, therefore, Hitler personally led loyal SS troops in a bloody purge of the SA. More than 150 senior SA figures were shot by firing squads. Many shouted "Heil Hitler!" prior to being executed for they had no idea why they were being shot. Röhm himself refused the revolver left in his cell, and two SS guards were forced to shoot him dead.

Many Nazis and non-Nazis with no connection to Röhm were also shot in the days following the "Night of the Long Knives" (or *Nacht der langen Messer*), as Nazis close to Hitler took the opportunity to settle old scores. For instance, Hermann Göring, jealous of the rank and influence of General

Jewish businesses were targets. Those not destroyed were "appropriated" and passed on to "Aryans."

Storm troopers pass notices with stereotypical Jewish images. Der Stürmer, a weekly Nazi newspaper, used such images as part of its anti-Semitic crusade. It was the only newspaper that Hitler read from cover to cover.

Kurt von Schleicher, had the retired general shot. The men sent to do the job also shot his wife dead and threatened his 14-year-old stepdaughter that she would suffer the same fate if she informed on them. In Munich the 75-year-old Gustav Ritter von Kahr, who had crushed Hitler's "Beer Hall Putsch" in 1923, was dragged from his home and beaten to death. His dismembered body was left in a swamp. There were many mistakes in the confusion. Willi Schmid, a respected music critic, was confused with a different Willi Schmidt and died as a consequence. Hitler's number two, Rudolf Hess, subsequently visited Frau Schmid to give her a pension and to tell

her to think of her husband's death as a "great sacrifice."

After all the killing had died down, Hitler concluded with the chilling words: "In this hour I was responsible for the fate of the German people, and therefore I became the Supreme Justice of the German people.... Everyone must know that in all future time if he raises his hand to strike at the state, then certain death will be his lot." Wilhelm Frick, the Reich Minister of the Interior, then framed an extraordinary law that declared all Hitler's actions during the purges to be legal. A compliant Reichstag passed the law without comment. The "Night of the Long Knives," conducted against former comrades, proved the ruthlessness of the new regime and was a foretaste of the terror to come. For those who were on the left of politics, those considered racially inferior, or those deemed in some way socially unacceptable, an equally severe fate awaited.

The fate of Alois Pfaller, a member of the German Communist Party, was typical of many. While most Communists kept their heads down once the Nazis achieved power, in 1934 Pfaller restarted his old Communist youth group. This was a heroic act, but one that was doomed to failure against a regime as ruthless as that of the Nazis. Pfaller was betrayed by a female double-agent—an agent working for both the Nazis and the Communists—and subsequently taken in by the Gestapo. In prison Pfaller was severely beaten and badly maltreated. His nose was broken and he was beaten unconscious with leather belts: "And when I came to again, they did it a second time, again unconscious, the fourth time, again unconscious, then they stopped because I hadn't said anything." The Gestapo then changed their interrogation techniques. One man took his confession down while another repeatedly hit Pfaller in the face every time he failed to answer a question correctly. The policeman doing the hitting sprained his right hand and began using his left. In the process he split Pfaller's eardrum: "Then I heard an incredible racket…. It was roaring as if your head was on the seabed, an incredible roaring." Pfaller then hemorrhaged and was given a bucket and mop and ordered to clean up his blood off the floor. Subsequently he was placed in a cell and then a concentration camp where he languished until 1945.

Anti-Semitism

The Jews became a prime target as racial doctrines in Nazi Germany were codified in a series of laws and spurious theories. However, Nazi policies toward the Jews varied through the 1930s. There were a series of uncoordinated attacks after the election of 1933. In Würzburg, a Jewish man was publicly humiliated and imprisoned for having an affair with a non-Jew. Jews were beaten

Reinhard Heydrich. Even after his death he caused suffering: in response to his assassination, the Germans destroyed the village of Lidice and massacred all the male inhabitants.

REINHARD HEYDRICH (1904–42)

Reinhard Heydrich was one of the most important figures in the Third Reich. He was a key architect of the Holocaust. He joined the Schutzstaffel (SS) in 1931 and founded the SS Security Service (SD). After the Nazis came to power in 1933, Heydrich rose rapidly through the ranks. He became the closest associate of SS head Heinrich Himmler.

In 1936, Heydrich became chief of the SD. In 1939 he assumed control of the Reich Security Main Office (RSHA). The office provided central control for SS and police terror activities in Germany and German-occupied territories. Heydrich organized the special SS and police mobile killing units (Einsatzgruppen). He also supervised the construction of the extermination camps.

At the Wannsee Conference in January 1942, Heydrich took charge of the "final solution to the Jewish question"—the Holocaust. On May 27, 1942, Heydrich was shot and bombed in his car by Czech partisans or guerrilla fighters. He died in Prague from his wounds.

by SA thugs brought into villages across Germany to attack Jewish families; Jews had their beards shorn or were forced to drink castor oil. Rudi Bamber's family was Jewish and lived in Nuremberg. In 1933 the SA arrived and "took my father away, and together with many other Jews in Nuremberg, they were taken to a sports stadium where there was a lot of grass and they were made to cut the grass with their teeth by sort of eating it.… It was designed to humiliate them, to suggest that they were the lowest of the low, and simply to make a gesture."

Soon the Nazis organized boycotts of Jewish shops. Premises were daubed with paint, and storm troopers would stand outside to intimidate any shoppers still willing to give them their business. In 1935 the Nuremberg Laws codified Nazi anti-Semitism. Jews were stripped of German citizenship and forbidden to marry "Aryans." Pressure on Jews eased up temporarily in 1936 and 1937 after protests from Schacht, Minister of Economics, worried about the economic consequences of persecuting Jews, and because of the Olympic Games being held in Berlin in 1936. But the underlying racial hatred remained.

Throughout the 1930s, Jews were forced from businesses and subjected to boycotts. Arnon Tamir's father ran a cigarette factory. Soon he was having problems because the town's cigarette dealers, with whom he had always had good relations, were unable to sell his cigarettes. Within two months of this boycott, his factory was forced to close down. In professions like the civil service, legislation was passed that prohibited Jews from employment.

Brownshirts parade through a German town. These same Brownshirts were used to attack Jews, wreck Jewish stores, and prevent customers from entering Jewish businesses.

Arnon Tamir grew up in a fearful atmosphere of anti-Semitism. This tainted his attitude to non-Jewish German girls: "The mere idea of becoming friendly, or more, with a German girl was poisoned right from the start by those horrible cartoons and headlines which claimed that the Jews were contaminating them." Nazi cartoons in the popular press played on the salacious dimension by portraying Jewish men as lecherous fiends intent on seducing innocent German girls. When Tamir worked on a building site, he overheard one Nazi Party member claim that a Jewish woman in his village was a sorceress. She was able, it was claimed, to turn herself into a foal. Such crude anti-Semitism had been a thread running through European society for centuries. However, it was now actively encouraged by the government of a well-organized modern state.

In 1938, the Nazis' persecution of the Jews exploded in *Kristallnacht* (Night of Broken Glass). Following the assassination of a German diplomat in Paris by a Polish Jew, Joseph Goebbels asked Hitler if he could release his storm troopers against Germany's Jewish population. Hitler agreed to the request, and on November 9 the attacks began. Across Germany the homes of Jews were raided. For the Bamber family, the first they knew of *Kristallnacht* was when Nazi thugs broke down their door. Storm troopers proceeded to smash up their apartment. The police did nothing: after all, the men doing the damage were themselves in uniform. "We had three elderly ladies who were living on the first floor with us," recalled Rudi Bamber, a boy at the time. "One was dragged out and beaten up, for no reason except she got in the way or something. And I was knocked around and finally ended up in the cellar.... A great many

people were arrested that night, and it was obviously their intention to arrest me as well. But after a while they found that the leader of the group had gone home. He had obviously had enough and they were very irritated by this. They weren't going to waste any more time, so they gave me a swift kick and said 'Go away'... and they walked out and left me to it." When Rudi reentered his apartment he discovered his father dying from the beating administered by the Nazis: "I was absolutely in shock. I couldn't understand how this situation had arisen ... uncalled-for violence against a people they didn't know."

Hitler and Röhm. The latter was seen by Hitler as being a threat by 1934, and was assassinated by SS men loyal to the Führer in the "Night of the Long Knives."

Once in power, the Nazis were ruthless with all genuine or imagined opponents. This is a photograph from the "Night of the Long Knives."

Ordinary people went along with this appalling violence against fellow Germans. One remembered that while *Kristallnacht* was a shock: "When the masses were shouting 'Heil' what could the individual person do? You went along. We went along. That's how it was. We were the followers." This line of argument does not, however, explain away the behavior of those in Nuremberg who went to the Bambers' house the morning after *Kristallnacht* and threw stones at the windows. At the end of *Kristallnacht*, more than 1,000 synagogues were destroyed and up to 400 German Jews had been killed. The broken glass littering the sidewalks of German cities on the morning of

Adolf Eichmann fled to Latin America after the war but was captured by Israeli agents.

ADOLF EICHMANN (1906–62)

Born in the Rhineland, Adolf Eichmann spent his youth in Linz, Austria. In 1932, he joined the Austrian Nazi Party. In 1934, he was sent to Berlin to work in the Security Service (SD) under Reinhard Heydrich. He joined the newly established Jewish Affairs Department in 1935 and became a specialist in the emigration of German Jews. By 1939 Eichmann was handling forced deportations to Poland.

In December 1939, Eichmann was transferred to the Gestapo as part of the Reich Security Main Office. He ran the headquarters for the implementation of the "Final Solution." In 1941 he began building death camps. He helped develop techniques for gassing prisoners. He also organized the transportation of victims to the camps from throughout the Reich. In August 1944, Eichmann reported to Heinrich Himmler, head of the SS, that approximately four million Jews had died in the death camps. He said that another two million had been killed by mobile extermination units.

After the war, Eichmann escaped to Argentina. He was caught there by Israeli agents in 1960. In 1961 he was tried in Israel for war crimes. He was hanged in May 1962.

November 10 gave this outburst of violence its name. World opinion was shocked by the events. The Americans withdrew their ambassador and a boycott of German goods intensified. But world opinion could do little for Germany's isolated Jewish community.

After this pogrom, the position for Germany's Jews went from bad to worse. Discriminatory laws were passed with the objective of creating a "Jewish-free" economy. Jews were now forbidden to practice trades or to own shops, market stalls, or businesses. Jewish businesses were "Aryanized"— that is, they were compulsorily sold to German non-Jews. Subsequently, Jews were banned from schools, universities, movie theaters, theaters, and sports facilities. Specific areas of cities were designated "Aryan" and forbidden to Jews. Local Germans zealously enforced these laws, and by the time war broke out in 1939 the Jews were becoming outsiders in German society.

These harsher policies coincided with Schacht's dismissal as Minister for Economics. Schacht had done something to temper the worst excesses of the Nazis, if only on the grounds that anti-Semitic policies harmed the German economy. Once Göring was in charge he aimed to create a "Jew-free" economy as quickly as possible. This coincided with events such as *Kristallnacht*. Anti-Jewish policies were also a result of intrigues at the highest levels of the Nazi decision-making process. For instance, Goebbels was eager to ingratiate himself with Hitler after news leaked of his various extramarital affairs: *Kristallnacht* was a means to curry favor with the Führer.

Hitler never swerved from his anti-Semitism. As war clouds gathered in

One of the slogans of Julius Streicher, owner of Der Stürmer *and Gauleiter of Franconia: "The Jews are our Ruin." It was typical of Nazi anti-Semitism.*

HEINRICH HIMMLER

Himmler ran the SS and the Gestapo, and his direct subordinates carried out the killings of the Holocaust.

Born in 1900, Heinrich Himmler took part in the failed Munich Putsch of 1923, and then became part of the Nazi Party's SS organization in 1925. He rose to lead the SS by 1930, and expanded it greatly. By 1933 it was 52,000 strong. After the Nazi Party took power, Himmler took over much of the police and security forces of Germany. In 1934, he was a key participant in the "Night of the Long Knives," when Hitler turned on and murdered some 1,000 of his former associates.

Himmler seems to have believed in a mixed set of ideas about the superiority of the Aryan race, and the need to get back to an idealized German existence based on farming. These chimed well with Hitler's racist attitudes, and Himmler was always part of the inner circle of Nazi leaders. His key subordinate was Reinhard Heydrich, who was made head of the Gestapo in 1934.

Himmler ran the Nazi concentration camp system, opening the first camp at Dachau in 1933, and the SS operated the camps. His racist beliefs, particularly that Slavs and Jews were *Untermensch* (subhuman), made it easy for him to order the mass killings that became part of the system after war broke out.

Himmler presided over a whole series of racist decrees—such as that "racially valuable" children were to be stolen from eastern Europe—and a complex ranking system for European "races" in which Norwegians were superior to the French, for example. He believed he could create a purely "Nordic" German race within generations of winning the war.

Himmler was a core part of the leadership that took the decision to wipe out the Jewish people in the Soviet Union by using killing squads after the invasion of June 1941, and the decision to use gas to murder millions in the death camps from 1942 onward.

Himmler visits Waffen-SS troops in the icy wastes of Finland. German troops served with the Finns against the Soviets until 1944.

Himmler with Ernst Kaltenbrunner (the man on the right with a scar), who had succeeded Reinhard Heydrich as the head of the Reich Central Security Office. In late 1944, Kaltenbrunner began to conspire against Himmler as part of the infighting that followed the failure of the July Plot to assassinate Hitler.

Himmler wipes his brow while visiting the Auschwitz death camp in 1942. He actively encouraged the Holocaust, believing it to be essential: "I am now referring to the evacuation of the Jews, to the extermination of the Jewish People," he said in a speech in 1943.

4. Himmler with his wife Margarete, who was seven years his senior. They married in 1928, and Margarete encouraged his interest in fringe medicine (such as homeopathy) and in creating a life as a subsistence farmer.

5. Himmler inspects a field position occupied by Waffen-SS troops. The Waffen ("fighting") SS grew out of the security role of the SS. Although regarded with suspicion by the regular army, the Waffen-SS grew into a huge force of over one million men, recruited from all over Europe. After an unpromising start, SS units fought well on many fronts. In spite of his extreme racism, Himmler was prepared to allow "subhuman" Slavs to serve in the Waffen-SS.

6 A group of senior Waffen-SS officers accompany Himmler during an inspection in 1944. By this time Himmler controlled 165 labor camps and 20 concentration camps. He was also the commander-in-chief of Army Group Upper Rhine, even though his military qualifications were slight.

6

Europe in 1939, he told an enthusiastic Reichstag: "[If] International Jewish finance inside and outside of Europe succeeds in involving the nations in another war, the result will not be the Bolshevization of the earth and the victory of Judaism but the annihilation of the Jewish race in Europe." At the same time, Hitler told the Czech foreign minister: "We are going to destroy the Jews. They are not going to get away with what they did on November 9th, 1918." This was a reference to the myth that Jews and Marxists forced Germany's surrender in November 1918.

In addition to persecution, the Nazis embarked on a policy to encourage Jewish emigration. As early as 1934, a subsection of the SS proposed to solve the "Jewish question" by pursuing an orderly and systematic policy of mass emigration. This was, however, not very successful: only 120,000 of Germany's 503,000 Jews had left by 1937. When Austria was annexed in 1938, 190,000

Wilhelm Frick, Reich Minister of the Interior after 1933. Frick was responsible for the Nuremberg Laws of 1935 that made Jews second-class citizens.

Austrian Jews were added to the Third Reich. This increase appalled the Nazis, who forced 45,000 to leave within six months by a policy of forced confiscation of Jewish property. This campaign was led by Adolf Eichmann, who fled to South America after the war, but was taken by Israeli agents in 1960, put on trial in Israel in 1961, and subsequently executed. In 1937, Eichmann had actually visited Palestine to meet Arab leaders as a means of speeding up Jewish settlement. In 1939, a further 78,000 Jews were forced out of Germany and 30,000 from recently annexed territory in Czechoslovakia. In an effort to find countries willing to accept these Jewish migrants, the Nazis even worked with Zionist organizations eager to establish a Jewish state outside Europe.

It was during the 1930s that the Nazis established concentration camps. The term "concentration camp" was first used in the context of the 1899–1902 South African War (or "Boer War"), in which British troops "concentrated" Afrikaner women and children to stop them from helping Boer fighters. Some 20,000 women and children died in the camps as a result of neglect by the British authorities. When Hitler came to power, he looked with interest at a different type of concentration camp for Germany. In a talk with a confidant before he became chancellor, Hitler stated: "We must be ruthless! We must regain our clear conscience as to ruthlessness. Only thus shall we purge our people of their softness and sentimental philistinism … and their degenerate delight in beer-swilling. We have no time for fine sentiments. I don't want the concentration camps transferred into penitentiary institutions. Terror is the most effective instrument. I shall not permit myself to

The official boycott of Jewish shops began in April 1933. In 1937, Jewish businesses could be confiscated without legal justification.

be robbed of it simply because a lot of stupid bourgeois mollycoddlers choose to be offended by it."

With this in mind, concentration camps were quickly established once the Nazis were in power. The avowed goal was to "reform" political opponents and turn antisocial elements into useful members of society. This was nonsense. On February 28, 1933, a law was passed suspending those clauses of the German constitution that guaranteed personal liberties. Three concentration camps were then established: Dachau in the south near Munich, Buchenwald in central Germany, and Sachsenhausen near Berlin. The first inmates were Jews and Communists, but soon Socialists, Democrats, Catholics, Protestants, pacifists, Jehovah's Witnesses, clergymen, and even dissident Nazis filled the camps. To meet the demand, other camps were established: Ravensbrück, Belsen, Gross-Rosen and Papenburg. Once Austria

was annexed, Mauthausen was built, and then Theresienstadt in Bohemian Czechoslovakia in 1939. After the conquest of Poland, extermination camps in the East were then constructed to carry out the "Final Solution."

Conditions in the concentration camps in the 1930s were brutal in the extreme. SS guards, selected from the worst elements of the Nazi movement, worked the starved and beaten inmates beyond their limits of physical endurance. Torture was commonplace. Inmates were divided into four groups: political opponents of Nazism; those deemed to be racially inferior; criminals; and "shiftless" elements believed to be antisocial. The second group (of those deemed racially inferior) was marked out for special treatment. Criminals were divided into two groups: the *Befristete*

Once the war began, German anti-Semitism expanded into occupied Europe. This is a picture from an anti-Jewish exhibition in Paris held in 1941.

THE HOLOCAUST

Away from the battlefields and the world's gaze, a hidden tragedy was taking place. Millions of innocents were being murdered by Nazis in the name of racial purity.

The Holocaust is the name given to the Nazi attempt to exterminate the Jewish race. An estimated six million Jews died. There were also hundreds of thousands of non-Jewish victims, mainly in Poland and Russia. They included Gypsies (Roma), homosexuals, Communists, and the mentally ill. The Nazis carried out much of the killing in extermination camps. The Holocaust is an example of genocide, or the attempted annihilation of a race. When Hitler and the Nazis first came to power in Germany in 1933, it seemed very likely that he would make life difficult and unpleasant for Germany's large Jewish community, but few expected the genocide that took place.

Vorbeugungshäflinge—or *BV*—(prisoners in limited-term preventive custody) were those who had already been in prison; the *Sicherungsverwahrte*—or *SV*—(prisoners in security custody) were convicts actually serving sentences. The political opponents were a spectrum of German society, from listeners of illegal radio stations to those actively opposed to the Third Reich. The "shiftless" element included homosexuals, who were subject to castration experiments to "correct" their sexual orientation.

All the inmates wore a colored patch on the left breast and right leg of their clothing. In addition, at many camps a serial number was tattooed on the left forearm. All political prisoners had a red patch; criminals, green; the "shiftless," black; homosexuals, pink; Gypsies, brown; and for Jews there were two yellow triangles that together formed a six-pointed Star of David. Foreigners in the camps were identified by letters: "F" for France, "P" for Poland. The letter "A" marked out a labor disciplinary prisoner (from the German word *Arbeit* for "work"). Those deemed "feeble-minded" were marked with *Blöd* ("stupid"). Inmates deemed an escape risk had to wear a red-and-white target sewn on the chest and back of their clothing.

Few groups within Germany, with the exception of the Jews, were treated with more brutality than the Gypsies. Two major groups of Gypsies, the Sinti and Roma, had migrated to Germany in the fifteenth century. While many had converted to Christianity, this did not protect them from persecution. Everything about them seemed wrong to the Nazi-sympathizing German: they were often scruffy, they were nomadic, and their customs and language singled them out from the surrounding German population. According to the Nazis' new racial science, they were habitual thieves and criminals. For these reasons, Gypsies were quickly rounded up and sent to the concentration camps. In September 1939, at a conference in Berlin chaired by Heydrich, a genocide program for the Gypsies was agreed upon, and they began to be murdered in the camps.

Paragraph 175 of the Reich Criminal Code, dating back to 1871, specified that sexual relations between men was a criminal act punishable by prison. This law was not as harshly enforced during the period of the Weimar Republic, and in the 1920s Hitler had turned a blind eye to the homosexuality of some of his followers; most famously, Röhm was an active homosexual. However, once Röhm's name was blackened following the "Night of the Long Knives," Hitler gave his support to the harshest treatment for homosexuals. Himmler, the head of the SS, proclaimed that any SS man found to be a homosexual would be "sent on my instruction to a concentration camp and shot while attempting to escape." Himmler was also responsible for establishing a central registry of all known homosexuals and an office to combat homosexuality. In the late 1930s, persecution speeded up and some 15,000 homosexuals were sent to concentration camps, where many of them were humiliated, tortured, castrated, and killed.

"Asocials"

In an effort to criminalize certain behavior, in 1938 the Reich Criminal Office defined "asocial" in the most general way as anyone who did not fit into the so-called people's community (the *Volksgemeinschaft*). This included tramps, Gypsies, beggars, prostitutes, alcoholics, and anyone who was "work-shy" (*arbeitscheu*), a drifter, or eccentric. With this catch-all classification, the Nazis could label someone "asocial" and send them off to the camps. With the Law for Prevention of Progeny with Hereditary Diseases, the helpless "asocial" could even be sterilized. There was little chance of rehabilitation, only imprisonment and death.

The mentally ill were also singled out for "special" treatment. The Nazis had long wanted to eradicate them, but public opinion was sufficiently strongly against it to prevent any "euthanasia" program (Christians and the various German churches were particularly prominent in this opposition). In 1935 Hitler told the Reich's leader of

Following the Anschluss with Germany, Viennese Jews are forced to clean the streets of the city. The Nazis tapped into a rich vein of anti-Semitism in Austria.

AUSCHWITZ

The arrival of
Hungarian Jews
at Auschwitz in
June 1944.

Auschwitz was the most infamous death camp. It was built by the Nazis in 1940 near the town of Oswiecim, Poland. At first, Auschwitz operated as a concentration camp. Most of its prisoners were Poles.

In the summer of 1941, the Nazis built a new extermination camp nearby, named Birkenau, or Auschwitz II. It had direct rail links with Berlin, Vienna, Warsaw, and Krakow for the transportation of prisoners. The new camp had gas chambers and crematoria for burning the bodies. The victims were gassed with a pesticide named Zyklon B. More than a million people are thought to have died at Auschwitz.

The camp complex also incorporated Auschwitz III, or Monowitz. This camp supplied forced labor for factories and workshops. When Auschwitz was abandoned in January 1945, the Nazis marched 58,000 inmates to other camps. Only a few survived to be liberated.

physicians, Dr. Wagner, that large-scale killing of the mentally ill would have to wait until wartime, when it would be easier to administer. But then, in 1938, a petition reached Hitler from a father who requested that the life of his deformed son be ended. Officials in the Chancellery of the Führer, headed by Philip Bouhler, had decided that this petition should be passed on to Hitler rather than be dealt with by a ministry official. Hitler then handed the decision to one of his personal doctors, Karl Brandt, who created a Reich Committee for the Scientific Registration of Serious Hereditary and Congenital Illness. This body served as an organizing force for reports sent in by doctors, nurses, and midwives across Germany wanting to know what to do with deformed children. These reports were scored by three doctors with a red plus sign (for death), a blue minus sign (for survival), or a question mark

MEDICAL EXPERIMENTS

Nazi doctors used inmates of concentration camps for a series of horrifying experiments. Among other tests, they deliberately exposed inmates to severe cold to study the effects of hypothermia. They wanted to learn how to protect German soldiers and airmen from freezing to death. Nazi doctors wanted to discover how long it took a body to freeze to death. They also wanted to try different ways to resuscitate a frozen victim.

Victims were plunged in ice water or left outside naked in subzero temperatures.

The Nazis also experimented with genetics. They wanted to prove the superiority of the Nordic or Aryan race. The most notorious name associated with such experiments was Joseph Mengele. Mengele was the chief doctor at Auschwitz. He killed inmates in order to carry out research on racial differences.

(for further assessment). The children marked with red were then killed with a lethal injection.

The mentally ill

Gerda Bernhardt's family was one of the thousands to suffer from this "euthanasia" policy.

Gerda's younger brother, Manfred, was intellectually disabled. When he was 10 he could say little beyond "Mum" and "Dad," and "Heil Hitler"—something he was proud to be able to pronounce. Neighbors suggested that it would be best if Manfred was "put away," but Manfred's mother resisted. Eventually, under pressure from her husband, Manfred's mother agreed to send Manfred to a children's hospital in Dortmund called Aplerback. Herr Bernhardt consoled his wife with the thought that Manfred would be put to work with animals on the hospital farm.

> "The children knew that those selected for 'immunization' were never seen again."

Manfred's family visited every two weeks, all that was allowed, but soon discovered that their son was becoming weak and apathetic. Shortly afterward, he died. The hospital authorities said that Manfred had died from natural causes, but when Gerda went to see the body she discovered many other small bodies covered in white sheets in the hospital morgue.

What was happening at Aplerback? Paul Eggert was the son of a violent, drunken father and, after being sterilized at the age of 11, was sent to the hospital at Aplerback as a "delinquent." He was there at about the same time that Manfred died. As he was not mentally ill, he carried out chores around the hospital. Eggert recalled pushing children's bodies around the hospital and how Dr. Weiner Sengenhof, one of the hospital's senior doctors, would "select" children at mealtimes for an immunization injection. The children knew that those selected for "immunization" were never seen again. One child clung on to Eggert outside the consultation room screaming for help as a nurse pulled him into the room. Later in life, Eggert recalled how: "These pictures would swim in front of my eyes when I lay in bed at night and they are still before my eyes today." Dr. Theo Niebel, the doctor in charge of the Special Children's Unit at Aplerback, remained in his post until his retirement in the 1960s.

Similar programs were instituted for mentally ill adults. At six selected asylums, specially trained teams of SS doctors and nurses prepared the way for the actual exterminations from late 1939. Adult patients were killed in gas chambers disguised as shower rooms or in mobile vans with carbon monoxide (often by the simple expedient of redirecting the exhaust fumes back into the locked van). Specially constructed crematoria then disposed of the corpses. News soon spread about these actions, and ugly scenes ensued as staff in some asylums sought to protect their patients from the SS. Relatives notified clergymen and judicial authorities. One judge who initiated criminal proceedings against Bouhler was promptly retired. These protests had some effect. Pressure from the upper echelons of the Catholic Church resulted in Hitler canceling the killings in August 1941, but not before 70,273 people had been killed. The methods of gassing for the mentally ill would be refined and extended

when the Germans looked for a "Final Solution" to the "Jewish problem."

What was the view of ordinary Germans on the use of terror against specific groups? It is a sad fact that there existed much popular approval when it came to the use of terror to deal with nonstandard behavior or nonstandard categories of people. The excuse of ignorance is not credible, as Nazi terror was highly visible, documented in the press and given legitimacy in the speeches of the Reich's leaders. Even some of those who criticized the regime or the detention and torture of political opponents approved of long prison sentences given to groups such

Rudolf Hess, deputy leader of the Nazi Party until his bizarre flight to Scotland in 1941, when he tried to negotiate a peace with Britain. He died in prison in 1987.

A German Jew is forced to wear the yellow Star of David. The wearing of yellow stars became compulsory for Jews living in Germany in September 1941.

as professional criminals, Gypsies, and homosexuals.

For most Germans, however, dissent was not an option. Their only response to what they must have guessed was happening was to shut their eyes to it. For the Nazis had taken measures to crush dissent soon after coming to power. Following the Reichstag Fire in February 1933 (the Reichstag building burnt to the ground in an arson attack that was a godsend to the Nazis, who used it to consolidate power), a decree was issued that suspended all civil liberties. This decree became constitutional law in March. In the same month, the Communist Party was banned. Slowly but surely the Nazis consolidated their iron grip. Hitler declared May Day a "Day of National Labor," and made it a paid holiday, something that many German workers had long desired. On May 2, however, the Nazis occupied union offices all over Germany using storm troopers in a well-planned and military-like operation; all workers' organizations were merged into the German Labor Front.

Seizing and maintaining control was not just a matter of passing laws and decrees, however; behind these measures was the use of terror. In the spring of 1933, units of the SA, SS, Gestapo, and police sealed off whole areas of towns and cities and combed them house by house (these operations were well planned, and often involved hundreds of personnel), searching for anything and anyone considered anti-Nazi, leaving no stone unturned. The raids were accompanied by threats, beatings, and arbitrary arrests. They created an atmosphere of fear and helplessness, and the subsequent buildup of the Gestapo surveillance system made resistance very difficult and dangerous.

Eyewitness Report:

" In Buna (Auschwitz) I worked for IG Farben making the Zyklon B gas that was used to gas the people. I was beaten and tortured at work, prayed to God at night not to wake up in the morning, and I wondered if I lived would there ever be a day when I would have enough bread to eat. I found a lump of dried bread in a box of machinery and I broke three teeth trying to break off small pieces to soften it and chew in my mouth. "

Joseph Kiersz, Polish inmate at Auschwitz, 1943

Roll call for the female inmates at Auschwitz–Birkenau. These women have had their heads shaved and would have been tattooed with a prison number.

CHAPTER 2
RACIAL WAR IN RUSSIA

In June 1941, Hitler invaded the Soviet Union. Close on the heels of the advancing German armies came the Einsatzgruppen, special SS squads whose task was to "cleanse" the newly conquered lands of Jews, Communists, and others who had no place in the Thousand Year Reich.

German soldiers hang Russian civilians in late 1941. Both the Einsatzgruppen and the Wehrmacht participated in executing "Jewish plunderers" or "Jewish Bolshevists"—largely catchall phrases.

Previous pages: Russian Jews forced to work for an SS Einsatzgruppe (special action group) during the early stages of Operation Barbarossa. Made to wear the Star of David, they would be shot after they had carried out their work duties.

The destruction of the Jews and other "unmentionables" who inhabited the Soviet Union was the avowed intention of Adolf Hitler. Shortly after the invasion of the Soviet Union he had stated: "This Russian desert, we shall populate it.... We'll take away its character of an Asiatic steppe, we'll Europeanize it... And above all, no remorse on this subject! We're absolutely without obligations as far as these people are concerned. To struggle against the hovels, chase away the fleas, provide German teachers, bring out newspapers—very little of that for us!" Hitler believed his dream of racial purity and the eradication of Bolshevism, which was in his eyes "a social criminality," was at hand. In fact what was really at hand for the peoples of the Soviet Union under German occupation was a period of brutality, exploitation, and extermination.

From the early 1920s Hitler was obsessed by the notion of *Lebensraum* (living space) for Germany at the expense of the Soviet Union. In *Mein Kampf* Hitler ominously wrote: "If we speak of soil in Europe today, we can primarily have in mind only Russia and her vassal border states.... For centuries Russia drew nourishment from the Germanic nucleus of its upper leading strata. Today it can be regarded as almost totally exterminated and extinguished. It has been replaced by the Jew.... He himself is no element of organization, but a ferment of decomposition. The giant empire in the East is ripe for collapse. And the end of Jewish rule in Russia will also be the end of Russia as a state." Nearly 20 years later the Führer was at last in a position to wage a racial-biological war against the "Jewish-Bolshevik intelligentsia."

The agents of the racial war

But such a special mission required special men. Hitler realized that the extermination of the Jews in the East was no undertaking for regular soldiers. Therefore, Reichsführer-SS Heinrich

Himmler was ordered to form special units to follow the German armies into the Soviet Union to undertake "special actions." These units were called Einsatzgruppen (special action groups).

During the invasion of the Soviet Union, Hitler granted Himmler special powers over the occupied territory in the East. On March 3, 1940, Himmler took responsibility for "certain tasks that stem from the necessity finally to settle the conflict between the two opposing political systems." The *Instructions on Special Matters* of March 13, 1941, divided occupied Russia into "ethnographic areas," each of which was to be ruled by a Reichskommissar.

Reinhard Heydrich, head of the SS Reich Main Security Office (RSHA) and Himmler's deputy, quickly worked out the areas of responsibility between the army and the Einsatzgruppen during Barbarossa. This task was simplified as far as the SS was concerned when Hitler's Commissar Order placed Communist commissars and officials, both military and civilian, beyond any law save one that automatically sentenced them to summary execution. Commissars when captured would be shot out of hand, if not by German frontline troops, then by the Einsatzgruppen, to whom they would be handed over: "Political leaders and commissars who are captured will not be sent to the rear."

On the eve of Barbarossa it had been established that "the Einsatzgruppen are authorized, within the framework of their task and on their own responsibility, to take executive measures affecting the civilian population." There were four Einsatzgruppen: Einsatzgruppe A, assigned to operations in Latvia, Lithuania, and Estonia, was commanded by SS-Gruppenführer Franz Stahlecker; Einsatzgruppe B, assigned to the Baltic

states and the Ukraine, was commanded by SS-Gruppenführer Arthur Nebe; Einsatzgruppe C, assigned to the Ukraine south of Einsatzgruppen B, was led by SS-Oberführer Carl Rasch; and Einsatzgruppe D, which assumed responsibility for the remainder of the Ukraine, was commanded by SS-Gruppenführer Otto Ohlendorf.

Units of the Sicherheitsdienst or SD (SS Security Service), Waffen-SS, and Ordnungspolizei (Order Police, or the regular uniformed police) provided men for the Einsatzgruppen, which were forces that were armed with light automatic weapons. The strength of

These Jews were murdered in the Ukrainian town of Lemberg in 1941. An SS NCO once stated: "What can they be thinking? I believe each still has the hope of not being shot. I don't feel the slightest pity."

the various Einsatzgruppen varied. Einsatzgruppe A had 990 men, while Einsatzgruppe D numbered 500.

Categories of victims

The atrocities began as soon as Barbarossa started. At the village of Virbalis, for example, Jews were forced to lie down and were then shot. The children were spared being shot, but were subsequently buried alive. The Einsatzgruppen took to their task with relish. They had been instructed by Heydrich: "Communist functionaries and activists, Jews, Gypsies, saboteurs, and agents must basically

be regarded as persons who, by their very existence, endanger the security of the troops and are therefore to be executed without further ado." In fact the list of those who were to be executed "without further ado" became all-encompassing: Russian commissars, Communists, looters, saboteurs, Jews with false papers, agents of the NKVD, traitorous ethnic Germans, "sadistic Jews," "unwanted elements," carriers of epidemics, members of partisan bands, armed insurgents, partisan helpers, rebels, agitators, young vagabonds, and Jews in general.

At first the Germans were welcomed as liberators, especially in the Baltic states and the Ukraine. But even as the troops were fraternizing, senior Nazis were putting in motion plans for the enslavement of the indigenous population.

Soon the Einsatzgruppen had murdered hundreds of thousands of people. Ohlendorf, for example, kept scores of his "achievements." By the winter of 1941–42, his group had liquidated 92,000 Jews alone. The wording of the reports of SS commanders made for chilling reading. On July 18, 1941, for example, SS-Obergruppenführer and General of the Waffen-SS and Polizei, Erich von dem Bach-Zelewski, Ordnungspolizei commander in the Soviet republic of Belorussia, sent the following to his superiors in Berlin: "In yesterday's cleansing action in Slonim, carried out by Police Regiment Center, 1,153 Jewish plunderers were shot." By August 7, he again reported, this time to SS-Oberstgruppenführer (General) and Generaloberst (Major General) of the Polizei, Kurt Daluege: "The total number of executions in the territory under my jurisdiction has now exceeded 30,000." The drive against the Jews was made easier because over 90 percent of Russian Jews were concentrated in Russia's cities. Einsatzgruppen tactics were to follow close behind the

advancing German troops and then seal off any town they came across.

Once the German Army had taken control of a town, the Einsatzgruppe commanders would move in and deviously go about their task. Jews were often tricked into surrendering themselves. In Kiev, for example, Einsatzgruppe C proudly reported that, "The Jewish population was invited

German troops in the Ukraine are welcomed by the locals. Hermann Göring, head of the Luftwaffe, stated: "The best thing would be to kill all men in the Ukraine over 15 years of age, and then to send in the SS stallions."

Hitler was particularly concerned that contact with the locals would lead to Slav women seducing young German soldiers and corrupting them away from the ideals of National Socialism.

Each SS man carried a "Soldbuch," a record of his personal details and SS activities. During Barbarossa many would record Einsatzgruppen assignments to undertake "resettlement measures" or "cleansing actions" against Jews; both were pseudonyms for mass killings. By mid-October the Einsatzgruppen had killed 300,000 Jews.

The image of its soldiers the SS liked to portray to the world. But the death's head insignia on the cap was a symbol of terror for the local population. Many SS personnel took great delight in sadistic murders as German rule spread. A favorite method was whipping unfortunate victims to death.

by poster to present themselves for resettlement. Although initially we had only counted on 5,000–6,000 Jews reporting, more than 30,000 Jews appeared: By a remarkably efficient piece of organization they were led to believe in the resettlement story until shortly before their execution."

The list of murders was endless: 4,200 Jews shot near the town of Kamenets-Podolsk; 1,255 Jews killed near the town of Ovruch; 12,361 Ukrainian Jews executed at the end of August 1941; in Lithuania, "about 500 Jews, among other saboteurs, are currently being liquidated every day"; and near Ogilev "a total of 135 people, most of them Jews, were seized, and 127 people were shot."

The murderers went about their task with a barbaric glee, smashing babies' heads against doors and stone walls, which one SS man remembered thus: "It went off with a bang like a bursting motorcycle tire."

However, even hardened fanatics have their limits, for by the winter of 1941–42 the Einsatzgruppen leaders were feeling the effects of the mass murders. Nebe had a nervous breakdown. In the hospital he ranted at his doctor: "Thank God, I'm through with it. Don't you

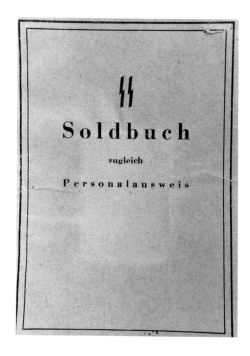

know what's happening in Russia? The entire Jewish population is being exterminated there." Nebe pleaded with Himmler to halt the murders, to be told by the Reichsführer: "That is a Führer order. The Jews are the disseminators of Bolshevism… If you don't keep your nose out of the Jewish business, you'll see what'll happen to you."

Alarmed by outbreaks of conscience among his henchmen, Himmler traveled to Minsk to encourage them. After attending the shooting of 200 Jews, which shocked him greatly, he told Nebe that a more efficient way of killing must be found. Nebe agreed, for the psychological effect on those who had to carry out the executions was very great. He began experimenting with killing people, in one case 80 inhabitants of a lunatic asylum, using exhaust gas from his car. He went about the task with an enthusiasm that he was incapable of keeping to himself. He was a keen amateur filmmaker and recorded his crude gas chamber on celluloid.

A like-minded individual was SS-Oberführer Christian Wirth, a former Stuttgart police officer who was an "expert" in experiments in mass sterilization. Wirth was eventually assigned to Poland, under Odilo Globocnik, head of the SS Jewish extermination program in Poland. Wirth's mission was to find an efficient method of dispatching one million Polish Jews. He selected an area along the Lublin–Lwow railway for his first experimental camp, and went on to head an organization of a group of four extermination camps.

Wirth focused his efforts on a stationary killing unit that had three "shower rooms," which was built at the center of the camp. Once inside, the victims were killed by the exhaust gas from diesel engines. He had wide doors on both the front and back walls to make the removal of gassed victims easier. The camp was able to murder

1,500 Jews daily. As they entered the gas chamber they saw a banner made from a synagogue curtain which stated in Hebrew: "This is the gate of the Lord into which the righteous shall enter."

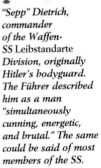

"Sepp" Dietrich, commander of the Waffen-SS Leibstandarte Division, originally Hitler's bodyguard. The Führer described him as a man "simultaneously cunning, energetic, and brutal." The same could be said of most members of the SS.

Nazi doctors, and also Reichsführer-SS Heinrich Himmler, were obsessed with racial differences in bone structure and the hereditary transmission of abnormalities. Any "suitable" guinea pigs, such as this little person photographed with police personnel, were sent to concentration camps for experimentation.

Himmler believed that Gypsies (such as the women pictured here) were capable of doing racial harm to his Nordic master race. Consequently, during Barbarossa German police units were ordered to round up Gypsies. Many were shot along with Jews. Later, Gypsies were sent to Auschwitz, to be housed in a separate enclosure before death.

A fellow SS officer noted in his journal the behavior of Wirth at the Belzec death camp in the aftermath of the gassing of a group of Jews: "Among it all the chief, Wirth, leaps about. He is in his element. Some workers check genitalia and backsides for gold, diamonds, and valuables. Wirth calls me over: 'Feel the weight of this tin of gold teeth—that is only from yesterday and the day before.'"

Once Barbarossa had finally stalled at the end of 1941, the Einsatzgruppen became static. They took over the existing auxiliary units or formed their own with recruits drawn from the ethnic Germans, pro-Germans in general, and reliable members of the defunct Soviet militia. They found many willing participants among the indigenous populations within German-occupied territory, and tapped into a rich vein of anti-Semitism. These units were often unreliable, poorly organized, ill-disciplined, and badly equipped and trained, but they could still take part in the hunting down and murder of Jews. In the Ukraine, for example, a Ukrainian Security Service in Cherson undertook guarding factories and stores against looters and saboteurs. Its tasks also included "the maintenance of peace," a euphemism for the rounding up of Jews.

At the end of 1941 the various Einsatzgruppen submitted their figures of Jews killed to Himmler: Einsatzgruppe A – 249,420; Einsatzgruppe B – 45,467; Einsatzgruppe C – 95,000; Einsatzgruppe D – 92, 000.

This figure of nearly 500,000 took place during the so-called "wild period" of Einsatzgruppen activities, when they followed hot on the heels of the German armies invading the Soviet Union.

The second period of SS rule in the Soviet Union was more organized though similarly brutal. Alfred Rosenberg was appointed Reich Minister for the Occupied Eastern Territories, being responsible for two Reich Commissariats—Ostland and Ukraine. Ostland consisted of Estonia, Latvia, Lithuania, and Belorussia. To carry out his orders, Himmler had appointed a number of Senior SS and Police (HSSPF) commanders in the occupied territories: SS-Gruppenführer Hans Prützmann as HSSPF North in Riga; SS-Gruppenführer Erich von dem Bach-Zelewski as HSSPF Center in Minsk; and SS-Obergruppenführer Freidrich Jeckeln as HSSPF South in Kiev. Later, in 1942, SS-Brigadeführer Gerret Korsemann was appointed HSSPF Caucasus. On Himmler's orders dated November 6, 1941, all auxiliaries were formed into auxiliary police units. These battalions were placed at the disposal of the order police commander and the HSSPF.

Systematically the Germans purged existing police and paramilitary

organizations and reformed them to suit their own needs. For example, all anti-Soviet partisans in and around Kovno, Lithuania, were disbanded on June 28, 1941, with five auxiliary companies subsequently formed from "reliable elements." The Jewish concentration

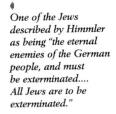

One of the Jews described by Himmler as being "the eternal enemies of the German people, and must be exterminated.... All Jews are to be exterminated."

Unusually, these auxiliaries are digging a grave themselves. Normally they would get their victims to dig a hole, after which they would be lined up on its edge and shot. This photograph suggests the victims were too weak to be able to dig the frozen soil.

An orthodox Jew is taunted by German troops. Einsatzgruppe commander Otto Ohlendorf stated: "I surrendered my moral conscience to the fact that I was a soldier.... I never permitted the shooting by individuals, but ordered that several men should shoot at the same time to avoid direct personal responsibility."

to 'hardness' and camaraderies, they reached a degree of insensibility surpassed only by those soulless automata, the concentration camp guards. Here was to be found the élite of that barbaric type of mankind, intoxicated by its own achievements, which Himmler exalted as the SS ideal; it was indeed an Order of the Death's Head, divorced from the world of ordinary mortals and from their moral standards, ready to undertake any mission ordered by its masters, and prisoner of a community claiming the sole right to decide the SS man's social and ethical standards.... Moreover, the deeds demanded of them took place in the vast expanses of Russia, so far distant from their normal environment that the whole murder business seemed like a dream ... so that what occurred had never really taken place."

The army's view

As the murders were taking place throughout German-occupied territory, many Wehrmacht commanders turned a blind eye to what was going on, or subsequently claimed that they had no knowledge of the atrocities being committed by the SS. After all, they argued, the delineation between army areas of responsibility and that of the SS was firmly established from the beginning of Barbarossa, and Himmler would brook no infringement on his sphere of influence. In this way, Wehrmacht personnel were able to distance themselves from the horrors being committed against the indigenous population. However, there is abundant evidence to prove that not only did army commanders know what was going on, but that they actively participated in Nazi ideological policy. The commander of the Sixth Army, Field Marshal Walther von Reichenau, part of Army Group South,

camp at Kovno was guarded by one company while another undertook police duties. In Wilna, the Lithuanian political police was disbanded in July 1941, with around 150 of its men being sent to the Einsatzgruppen. In Belorussia an auxiliary police unit was formed from Polish and Belorussian criminal police officials. All these units readily assisted in the roundup and extermination of Jews.

However, it was the Einsatzgruppen that committed the most murders in the Soviet Union. As the historian Heinz Höhne stated: "Wholly dedicated reacted to reports of the "softness" of his troops by instilling them with particularly strong statements about their role in suppressing Communism and Soviet Jewry. Von Reichenau was known as one of the most strongly Nazi of the leading German Army commanders. He died of a stroke only a few months after he issued the document below to his troops. Other German commanders in the Soviet Union also used this document to instruct their troops. The order was issued on October 10, 1941, entitled *Conduct of Troops in Eastern Territories.*

"Regarding the conduct of troops toward the Bolshevistic system, vague ideas are still prevalent in many cases. The most essential aim of war against the Jewish-Bolshevistic system is a complete destruction of their means of power and the elimination of Asiatic influence from the European culture. In this connection the troops are facing tasks which exceed the one-sided routine of soldiering. The soldier in the Eastern territories is not merely a fighter according to the rules of the art of war, but also a bearer of ruthless national ideology and the avenger of bestialities that have been inflicted upon German and racially related nations. Therefore, the soldier must have full understanding for the necessity of a severe but just revenge on subhuman Jewry. The Army has to aim at another purpose, i.e. the annihilation of revolts in the hinterland, which, as experience proves, have always been caused by Jews.

"The combating of the enemy behind the front line is still not being taken seriously enough. Treacherous, cruel partisans and degenerate women are still being made prisoners-of-war, and guerrilla fighters dressed partly in uniform or plain clothes and vagabonds are still being treated as proper soldiers, and sent to prisoner-of-war camps. In fact, captured Russian officers talk even

The treatment of the people of the Baltic states, many of whom were considered by the Nazis to be "Nordic" in racial characteristics, was more lenient than toward "subhumans." Many thousands of Estonians and Latvians joined the ranks of the Waffen-SS during the war.

The murderers take time to relax. It has been estimated that as many as 1,400,000 Jews had been murdered as a result of German Einsatzgruppen activities by the spring of 1942.

mockingly about Soviet agents moving openly about the roads, and very often eating at German field kitchens. Such an attitude of the troops can only be explained by complete thoughtlessness, so it is now high time for the commanders to clarify the meaning of the pressing struggle.

"The feeding of the natives and of prisoners-of-war who are not working for the armed forces from army kitchens is an equally misunderstood humanitarian act, as is the giving of

cigarettes and bread. Things that the people at home can spare under great sacrifices and things that are being brought by the command to the front under great difficulties, should not be given to the enemy by the soldier even if they originate from booty. It is an important part of our supply.

"When retreating, the Soviets have often set buildings on fire. The troops should be interested in the extinguishing of fires only as far as it is necessary to secure sufficient numbers of billets. Otherwise, the disappearance of symbols of the former Bolshevistic rule even in the form of buildings is part of the struggle of destruction. Neither historic nor artistic considerations are of any importance in the Eastern territories. The command issues the necessary directives for the securing of raw material and plants, essential for the war economy. The complete disarming of the civilian population in the rear of the fighting troops is imperative considering the long vulnerable lines of communications. Where possible, captured weapons and ammunition

A police detachment operating in German-occupied territory. Tens of thousands of locals were recruited by the Germans to implement Nazi policy in the conquered territories. Of little use militarily, they were often recruited from the worst elements of society. Murder and savagery came easily to them.

Gustav der Eiserne spricht:
„Je mehr Dienst
desto grösser die Ehre ist."

should be stored and guarded. Should this be impossible because of the situation of the battle, the weapons and ammunition will be rendered useless.

"If isolated partisans are found using firearms in the rear of the army drastic measures are to be taken. These measures will be extended to that part of the male population who were in a position to hinder or report the attacks. The indifference of numerous apparently anti-Soviet elements, which originates from a 'wait and see' attitude, must give way to a clear decision for active collaboration. If not, no one can complain about being judged and treated a member of the Soviet system. The fear of German countermeasures must be stronger than threats of the wandering Bolshevistic remnants. Regardless of all future political considerations the soldier has to fulfill two tasks:

"1. Complete annihilation of the false Bolshevist doctrine of the Soviet State and its armed forces.

"2. The pitiless extermination of foreign treachery and cruelty and thus

the protection of the lives of military personnel in Russia.

"This is the only way to fulfill our historic task to liberate the German people once and for all from the Asiatic-Jewish danger.

"[signed] von Reichenau"

In this way the Wehrmacht became actively involved in Nazi ideology in the East. The Germans had no military guidelines for combating partisan bands, and as the frustration of trying to battle

Jews are rounded up before being transported to a ghetto. The Jewish ghettos had been established by the Nazis during the winter of 1939–40, all of which quickly became overcrowded. By 1942 the Warsaw ghetto, which housed over 500,000 people, became so unhealthy that an average of 5,000 were dying there every month.

39

an elusive foe grew, a foe who often committed atrocities against isolated German patrols, reprisals became more widespread and indiscriminate.

Nazi racial policy had particularly disastrous consequences in the Ukraine, where many towns and villages had welcomed the Germans as liberators (it is estimated that up to seven million Ukrainians had died of starvation during Stalin's collectivization policies in the 1930s—the terror of Soviet Communism convinced many Ukrainians that they would be better off under the control of a cultured country such as Germany), only to discover the truth as the Wehrmacht conquered their land. For the "subhuman" inhabitants of the Ukraine, Hitler planned that they would "disappear." A few might be left as slave laborers to serve the German colonists. In this way the Germans alienated 40 million Ukrainians who might otherwise have aided the anti-Soviet war effort.

The historian George Stein summarizes the German war in the Soviet Union thus: "When the enemy is regarded as a repulsive and evil animal, an *Untermensch*, a subhuman, the result is an unmatched brutalization of warfare, for the soldier is generally set free from feelings of guilt or remorse for his grisly deeds…. The deplorable effects that resulted from the artificial dehumanization are well known—the shooting of prisoners, the murder of civilians, the destruction of peaceful villages." Such were the results of Hitler's racial crusade to save Western civilization against "Asiatic Bolshevism."

SPOTLIGHT

ANTI-JEWISH PROPAGANDA

Throughout Europe, the Nazi regime undertook a virulent campaign to spread its anti-Jewish message.

In 1933, when Hitler came to power, the Jewish community in Germany was 650,000 strong. It was fully assimilated into German society, and it made valuable economic and social contributions to Germany as a whole. Yet Hitler had expressed rabid anti-Semitism since his youth, and he presented a theory of a worldwide Jewish conspiracy that took root in Germany astonishingly easily.

The roots of European anti-Semitism lie in the medieval period, including beliefs about the sacrifice of Christian babies by Jews, for example; and even when legal restrictions against Jews were lifted during the nineteenth century, there was widespread discrimination and anti-Semitism throughout Western Europe, expressed in such episodes as the Dreyfus case in France or in daily issues such as the exclusion of Jews from membership of certain golf clubs in Great Britain.

What Hitler brought to the mix was a poisonous interpretation of "social Darwinism"—which itself was a way of applying Darwin's ideas of competition within species to different human societies—to

form a racial hierarchy, in which the white race was superior to blacks, Chinese, etc. Hitler used the ideas of social Darwinism to formulate a Jewish identity that was hostile to the "Aryan" race. The fact that the concept of human races in genetic terms was ridiculous—and particula[r] the idea of an "Aryan" race—did not seem to matter. Germany after 1919 was politically and socially fragmented, enduring events such as the great inflation of the mid-1920s that destroyed social cohesion. Raci[s] became acceptable, as the Nazi message was purveyed through all channels.

Attacks on Jews, both in new laws and in episodes of street violence suc[h] as Kristallnacht in 1937, escalated. Then, during World War II itself, propaganda increased with a series o[f] poster campaigns that justified and underpinned the Holocaust. As in al[l] successful conspiracy theories, the conspiracy could never be disproved. It was seen as all-consuming and all-powerful, and it was very much in the interests of the Nazi state to maintain the myth of their evil, secre[t] Jewish enemy.

Left: This poster was produced for France by the "French League," a right-wing organization with links to the Catholic Church led by Pierre Constantini. The message at the top reads: "France, watch out for ghosts!" The ghosts are Anglo-Saxon capitalism (with its bag of money), freemasons (with the square and compasses symbol), artists and left-wing intellectuals (with paintbrush), and behind these three, the big-nosed Jew.

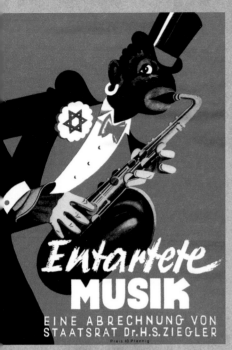

Above: "Degenerate music" is the message of this poster. It is a crude exaggeration of a 1927 jazz-influenced opera. The figure of a black musician wearing a Star of David became a Nazi symbol for anything they considered degenerate or non-Aryan in the arts.

Left: "Behind the enemy powers: the Jew" is the message of this Nazi poster, as a Jew moves shiftily behind the flags of Great Britain, the USA, and the USSR. Germany's main enemies were thus linked as part of the "Jewish conspiracy." Hitler had said of the Jews in 1938: "We know that they are representatives of an international anti-German movement and we shall treat them all accordingly."

Above: "He is guilty for the war!" screams this poster by the talented artist using the pseudonym Mjolnir (Mjolnir was the hammer of the Viking god of thunder, Thor). Nazi anti-Jewish propaganda was relentless during the 1930s and 1940s.

Above: Another Mjolnir poster, showing a curtain being pulled back to reveal a Jewish face above a burning, devastated landscape. The message reads: "The Jew: inciter of war and prolonger of war." Like all conspiracy theories, the message was never susceptible to rational analysis. Whatever arguments were used to refute anti-Semitism, there was always a further response in which Jews were the enemies of the German people.

Above: A Mjolnir poster that appeared in February 1943. "Victory or Bolshevism" read the words, and the message concerning the dreadful results of a Russian victory is clear. The Nazis had always linked Communism ("Bolshevism") to a Jewish conspiracy, and this poster does so by giving the face of the Bolshevik a Jewish nose. After the defeat at Stalingrad early in 1943 the Nazi Party's Central Propaganda Office issued the following directive: "For the time being, propaganda against the plutocratic Western powers will be secondary to the propaganda against Bolshevism.... Bolshevism is the main enemy we have to fight against, which is the most radical expression of the Jewish drive for world domination."

CHAPTER 3
GENOCIDE

In January 1942, at the Wannsee Conference, senior Nazis put in motion their plans for the "Final Solution of the Jewish question in Europe." The entire Jewish population of Europe was to be transported by rail to specially built death camps, where they would be gassed and their bodies disposed of in crematoria. Before Nazi Germany was defeated, six million Jews had been murdered.

In addition to the 10,000 unburied dead, the British found a mass grave containing 40,000 bodies in Belsen.

Previous pages: Belsen concentration camp after its liberation. More than half of the inmates died in the weeks that followed, of malnutrition, typhus, and dysentery.

"Let not the land cover up their blood." The monument to the victims of Belsen was erected outside the camp by British Jews in 1946.

In the winter of 1944 Christabel Bielenberg, wife of a member of the "Kreisau Circle," shared a railroad carriage with a young Latvian SS man who recounted his experiences in Poland: "Well, they told us that we could revenge ourselves on our enemies, and they sent us to Poland. Not to fight the Poles, oh no, they had been defeated long ago—but to kill Jews. We just had the shooting to do, others did the burying," he drew a deep, sighing breath. "Do you know what it means—to kill Jews, men, women, and children as they stand in a semicircle around the machine guns? I belonged to what is called an *Einsatzkommando*, an extermination squad—so I know. What do you say when I tell you that a little boy, no older than my youngest brother, before such a killing, stood there to attention and asked me 'Do I stand straight enough, Uncle?' Yes, he asked that of me; and once, when the circle stood round us, an old man stepped out of the ranks, he had long hair and a beard, a priest of some sort I suppose. Anyway, he came toward us slowly across the grass, slowly step by step, and within a few feet of the guns he stopped and looked at us one after another, a straight, deep, dark and terrible look. 'My children,' he said, 'God is watching what you do.'

He turned from us and then someone shot him in the back before he had gone a few steps. But I, I could not forget that look, even now it burns me."

The Latvian SS man was obviously deeply troubled by the terrible acts he had committed, yet at some level he remained a considerate human being. Bielenberg fell asleep in the carriage: "I awoke twice before reaching Tuttlingen. Once, when the train jerked to a stop at a half-lit station, I realized that I was warmer and that my head was resting on something hard and uncomfortable. The man had moved and was sitting beside me, he had placed his greatcoat over my knees and my head had fallen onto his shoulder. His SS shoulder tabs had been pressing into my cheek. In the half-light I saw his face for the second time: perhaps I had been mistaken about the twitching nerve; it looked peaceful enough, almost childlike.... The next time I woke, the carriage was empty and the train was moving."

There are disturbing questions raised by this account. How did ordinary men and women come to commit such crimes and, given the numbers involved in the extermination of the Jews, did the German public really not know what was happening to Europe's Jewish population?

Almost as soon as Hitler came to power the Nazis began to enact discriminatory legislation against Germany's Jews. The Nazi Party had pledged to create a Germany in which Jews would be set apart from their fellow Germans and denied their place in German life and culture. Jews were expelled from a number of smaller towns and forced to move to larger towns or cities, or emigrate. In the interwar years the Nazi state continued to exclude its Jewish population from mainstream life and encourage its

emigration out of Germany. During this period the mass murder of Germany's Jews was not envisaged. Indeed, the number of Jews who died in Germany's concentration camp system, designed to punish the opponents of the regime and that killed many thousands of Communists, Social Democrats, and other "undesirables," numbered fewer than 100 between 1933 and 1938. However, the level of violence increased as war approached. In November 1938, for example, 91 Jews were murdered on a night of burning and looting known as "The Night of Broken Glass." In the following six months the numbers of Jews dying in Germany's concentration camps began to increase.

Systematic slaughter
The outbreak of war led to a change in approach. Following the conquest of

Poland in 1939, German units began systematically murdering elements of the Polish intelligentsia, leaders, clergy, and also Polish Jews. Admiral Wilhelm Canaris, the anti-Nazi head of the German Military Intelligence Service, reported that SS commanders were boasting of 200 killings a day. Of the 10,000 Poles murdered, some 3,000 were Jews. This, however, was not part of a concerted plan of extermination. From spring 1940 the Germans began to concentrate Poland's Jews into ghettos in a number of major cities. A blatantly anti-Semitic population facilitated such treatment, far more extreme than anything so far experienced by German Jews. By 1941, the process of ghettoization was as complete as human ingenuity could make it, and despite a deliberate policy of food rationing, which led to starvation, the mass of

Jewish women sealed in cattle trucks on their way to Auschwitz. Few inside the so-called "Special Resettlement Trains" survived.

Kristallnacht, *"The Night of Broken Glass,"* November 9–10, 1938. The synagogue in Magdeburg after the night of Nazi looting and burning of Jewish property.

Polish Jews continued to survive in the ghettos.

The attack on the Soviet Union, however, led to an escalation of the persecution of Europe's Jews. Hitler warned his generals that the war would be fought on racial lines: "We are talking about a war of annihilation." Before the attack in June 1941, he issued the Commissar Order requiring the shooting of any Soviet commissars captured. The Einsatzgruppen, commanded by Reinhard Heydrich of the SS, were instructed to kill only "Jews in the service of party and State." However, there can be little doubt that the orders were interpreted as an instruction to kill all Jews. It led within six months to the murder of as many as one million Jews. They were killed in circumstances very similar to that described by the Latvian SS man in the opening quote. The Einsatzgruppen units numbered a mere 3,000 men, which raises the question of how they killed so many in such a

short period of time. The answer is that they required the collaboration of the army. When the Commissar Order was passed on to Hitler's commanders, few, if any, objected. General Hermann Hoth, commander of the Fourth Panzer Army, declared: "The annihilation of those same Jews who support Bolshevism and its organization for murder, the partisans, is a measure of self-preservation."

Shortly before taking command of the Eleventh Army, General von Manstein said that: "The Jewish-Bolshevik system must be rooted out once and for all." Field Marshal von Reichenau's order to the Sixth Army of October 10, 1941, clearly makes the Wehrmacht responsible for the atrocities against Jews in the Ukraine: "In this eastern theater of war, the soldier is not only a man fighting in accordance with the rules of war, but also the ruthless standard-bearer of national ideals and the avenger of all the bestialities perpetrated on the German peoples.

For this reason the soldier must fully appreciate the necessity for the severe but just retribution that must be meted out to the subhuman species of Jewry." His troops' duty was to "free the German people forever from the Jewish-Asiatic threat." When handling large populations, it was inevitable that the regular German troops were involved. Dorothea Schlösser, part of an entertainment troupe touring Wehrmacht groups, recalled: "Soldiers told me about the horrible things happening to the Jews while I was in Poland singing with a road show to entertain the troops. Everyone seemed to be talking about the truckloads of Jews who were being brought in and killed. The soldiers cried like children when they talked about it. I will never forget one experience I had while I was in Warsaw. I was standing off stage waiting for my appearance when I noticed some young soldiers in the audience. There were dancers on stage and one of the soldiers began to laugh hysterically and said, 'I already saw some people dancing tonight— the Jews we took away!' Then he suddenly began to sob, 'Why don't they defend themselves?'"

Not all were as traumatized as the young soldiers mentioned above. The Sixth Army was forced to issue the following instruction in August 1941: "In various places within the army's area of responsibility, organs of the SD, of the Reichsführer's SS, and chiefs of the German police have been carrying out necessary executions of criminal, Bolshevik, and mostly Jewish elements. There have been cases of off-duty soldiers volunteering to help the SD with their executions, or acting as spectators and taking photographs." Such orders prove the awareness of much of the Wehrmacht chain of command of

the policy of extermination. Despite the above instruction, troops continued to be involved in anti-Jewish actions. Antony Beevor explained why: "German soldiers were bound to mistreat civilians after nine years of the regime's anti-Slav and anti-Semitic propaganda, even if few of them consciously acted at the time out of Nazi values. The nature of the war produced emotions that were both primitive and complex. Although there were cases of soldiers reluctant to carry out executions, most natural pity for civilians was transmuted into

The SD *in action in Poland. In the wake of the German Army there came the* Einsatzgruppen, *which systematically began to murder sections of Polish society.*

Jews in France are rounded up for deportation to a concentration camp. The Germans deported and murdered 83,000 Jews from France alone.

an incoherent anger based on the feeling that women and children had no business to be in a battle zone."

Brave protest

Some did protest. Martin Koller, a Luftwaffe officer, had a very similar conversation to that of Christabel Bielenberg when returning by train from leave: "We talked about all kinds of things, everyday subjects, war, and private life. And then he said he'd taken part in shooting Jews somewhere in the Baltic. There had been more than 3,000 of them. They had to dig their own grave 'as big as a soccer field.' He told me this with a certain pride. I was completely at a loss and asked stupid questions like, 'Is it really true?' 'How was it done?' 'Who led this operation?'

And I got precise answers to each. It was true, anyone could check; with twelve men armed with machine pistols and one machine gun. The ammunition had been officially provided by the Wehrmacht, and a German SS lieutenant, whose name he didn't remember, had been in command. I became confused and started to sweat. This just didn't fit into the whole picture—of me, of my country, of the world, of the war. It was so monstrous that I couldn't grasp it. 'Can I see your identification?' I asked, and 'Do you mind if I note it down?' He didn't mind and was just as proud of what he had done as I was of the planes I had shot down. And while I scribbled his... name down on a cigarette package, my thoughts somersaulted: either what he's told me is true, in which case I can't wear a German uniform any longer, or he's lying, in which case he can't wear a German uniform any longer. What can, what should I do? My military instinct told me, 'Report it!'"

Koller did make a report and a senior officer quashed it. Yet there can be no doubt knowledge of the fate of the Jews did circulate, despite the regime's efforts to keep it secret. Conservative resister Helmuth von Moltke, a friend of Bielenberg's husband, spoke to a nurse from an SS sanatorium for men who had broken down shooting Jewish women and children. Racial policies and atrocities were discussed openly in military and governmental circles. Nor was the knowledge restricted to the small policy-making élites. The White Rose

group of Munich University students led by the Scholls included in one of their anti-Nazi pamphlets: "Since the conquest of Poland 300,000 Jews have have been murdered ... in the most bestial way. Here we see the most frightful crime against human dignity, a crime that is unparalleled in our whole history." Rumors abounded in Frankfurt and Berlin in the summer of 1943 that deported Jews were being gassed.

German authorities moved from the slaughter of Jews behind the lines on the Eastern Front to what was known as the "Final Solution" of the Jewish question. That solution, formalized at the Wannsee Conference in January 1942, was the extermination of all European Jewry. Jews living throughout Europe, whether confined to ghettos

Inside the Warsaw Ghetto. By 1941, the daily food ration in the ghetto was 184 calories, compared to 669 for a Pole and 2163 for a German.

in Poland or still living in their own homes, were to be rounded up and detained in local holding camps before being deported by train to distant camps where they would either be worked to death or murdered by gas. Such a large-scale undertaking had to draw upon a lot more than just military support. This enforced mass movement of Jews from Germany and elsewhere in Europe required the involvement of many civilians. The latter often later claimed to have had no knowledge of their role in the "Final Solution."

The following is a postwar interview with a senior railroad official (RO):
Why were there more special trains during the war than before or after it?

RO: I see what you're getting at. You're referring to the so-called resettlement trains.
Resettlement. That's it.
RO: That's what they are called. Those trains were ordered by the Ministry of Transport of the Reich. You needed an order from the ministry.
In Berlin.
RO: Correct. And as for the implementation of those orders, the Head Office of Eastbound Traffic in Berlin dealt with it.
Yes, I understand.
RO: Is that clear?
Perfectly. But mostly, at the time, who was being "resettled"?
RO: No! We didn't know that. Only

Jews are rounded up in the Warsaw Ghetto in 1943. When the Germans began to clear the ghetto in April 1943, they were met by extremely stiff resistance.

when we were fleeing from Warsaw ourselves, did we learn that they could have been Jews, or criminals, or similar people.

Jews, criminals?

RO: Criminals. All kinds.

Special trains for criminals?

RO: No, that was just an expression. You couldn't talk about that. Unless you were tired of life, it was best not to mention that.

But you knew that the trains to Treblinka or Auschwitz were...

RO: Of course we knew. I was the last district; without me these trains couldn't reach their destination. For instance, a train that started in Essen had to go through the districts of Wuppertal, Hanover, Magdeburg, Berlin, Frankfurt/ Oder, Posen, Warsaw, etc. So I had to...

Did you know that Treblinka meant extermination?

RO: Of course not!

You didn't know?

RO: Good God, no! How could we know? I never went to Treblinka. I stayed in Krakow, in Warsaw, glued to my desk.

You were a...

RO: I was strictly a bureaucrat!

I see. But it's astonishing that people in the department of special trains never knew about the "Final Solution."

RO: We were at war.

Because there were others who worked for the railroads who knew. Like the train conductors.

RO: Yes, they saw it. They did. But as to what happened, I didn't.

What was Treblinka for you? Treblinka or Auschwitz?

RO: Yes, for us Treblinka, Belzec, and all that were concentration camps.

A destination.

RO: Yes, that's all.

But, not death?

RO: No, no...

▲ *A concentration camp survivor sorts through a pile of rags after liberation. The killings continued until the camps were overrun by the advancing Allies.*

It is possible that this man was not lying and lacked the insight to conclude what his role was in the process of the "Final Solution." Given the rumors at the time and the fact that the trains never brought anyone back, it is reasonable to presume that German transportation officials, and there were many thousands of them, had some knowledge of what was going on. Recent historical studies, such as Daniel Goldhagen's *Hitler's Willing Executioners*, have persuasively argued this case. Transportation workers were not the only people involved. Doctors and nurses checked the Jews

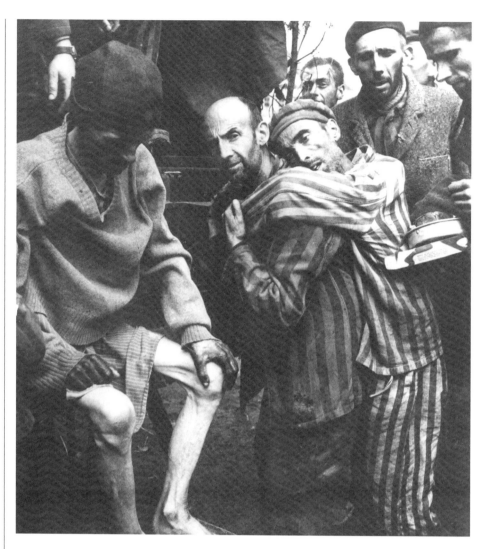

Some of the "lucky ones." Emaciated survivors of a concentration camp following their liberation in 1945. Many survivors, their bodies weakened by starvation and malnutrition, died in the weeks following their liberation.

before departure, and postal workers delivered the initial messages to German Jews ordering their deportation. Normal policemen were often responsible for roundups in Germany, and Jews were often moved through the streets in broad daylight in preparation for their deportation. Also, the examples of Christabel Bielenberg and Martin Koller prove there were plenty of those directly involved at the most brutal end of the process who were willing to talk about it. Although it was wise not to voice such tales too openly, there must have been many conversations in train carriages or bars as people tried to

unburden themselves. The most likely explanation seems to be that, even if much of the German population did not precisely and categorically know that the systematic extermination of the Jews was being undertaken, they still must have suspected that something was happening. The only conclusion is that, perhaps partially due to the penalties for nonconformism in Hitler's Germany, the vast majority of Germans were indifferent to the fate of the Jews who had been around them until recently.

As for those German Jews who were rounded up by their fellow Germans and sent aboard German-run trains to the

German-run death and concentration camps, a grim fate awaited them. "We had," Auschwitz commandant Rudolf Höss explained, "two SS doctors on duty to examine the incoming prisoners. These would be marched to one of the doctors, who would make spot decisions. Those who were fit to work were sent into the camp. Others were sent immediately to the extermination plants. Children of tender years were invariably exterminated, since by reason of their youth they were unable to work."

It was a terrifying ordeal for those who arrived at the death camps. The routine at Treblinka was similar to that in other camps. As soon as the cattle-wagon doors were unbolted the camp guards would use whips and dogs to herd those inside into the open. Men and women were separated, made to undress and then hand in their valuables. The old and infirm were led off toward the infirmary, but then arrived at a mass grave where each one was shot in the back of the head and thrown in. Men were sent to the gas chamber first as they took less time; women had to have their hair shorn in the chamber itself by a team of Jewish barbers working at a rate of two minutes per person. Then the doors to the chamber were closed.

Dr. Kurt Gerstein was a disinfection officer at Belzec and witnessed a "typical" gassing: "Even in death one knows the families. They squeeze each other's hands, clenched in death, so that there is difficulty tearing them apart in order to evacuate the chamber for the next consignment. The cadavers, damp with sweat and urine, legs splattered with excrement and blood, are hurled outside. Children's corpses fly through the air.... Two dozen dentists open the jaws with hooks and look for gold. Gold left, without gold right. Other dentists break the gold teeth and crowns from the jaws with pliers and hammers." Those that were "lucky" enough to pass the selection faced death through starvation and overwork, or even at the hands of the camp guards, who were mostly recruited for their indifference to suffering and their willingness to carry out the most inhumane orders. Dora Völkel recalled: "We were beaten a lot and hardly given anything to eat. You could watch human beings turn into animals. Many people lost all sense of human dignity.... We were forced to carry heavy rocks from one place to another. We had to carry a rock more than a half mile (1 km), set it down, pick up another rock, and carry that back to where we had originally come from. And of course, there was the fire, the bright fire rising from the chimney. You couldn't help but notice it. It burned night and day. People came from Hungary, and we said, 'Tonight the Hungarians are burning. When is it going to be our turn?'"

By April 1944 there were 13 parent camps and 500 sub-camps operating in German-controlled territory. The biggest

Ilse Koch, widow of the commandant of Buchenwald, on trial at Dachau for crimes against humanity in 1947, including having lampshades made of human skin.

THE HOLOCAUST

The concentration camp system killed people from all over Europe.

The Nazis began the organized killing of populations with German mentally ill patients: this began before 1939, and between 1939 and 1941 almost 100,000 are thought to have been killed.

The Jewish people of Europe suffered the most deaths. Of the prewar Jewish population of about 8,800,000, nearly six million were killed during World War II. The largest numbers were from Poland and the Soviet Union: three million (out of a pre-war population of 3,300,000) in Poland and 1,250,000 from the Soviet Union. Many Polish Jews were killed as part of a concerted policy of starvation after the German occupation of 1939; and in the Soviet Union attacks on Jews by special killing squads after the invasion of June 1941 accounted for many victims.

However, the death camps accounted for most of the Jews killed from other parts of Europe: for the 90,000 French Jews murdered, or the 450,000 Hungarian Jews who were the last major Jewish population of Europe to be killed. Some Jewish populations escaped relatively unscathed: the Danish Resistance, for example, managed to smuggle Denmark's Jews across to Sweden.

Other Jewish populations, however, were severely treated by their neighbors: in the Baltic States, only some 30,000 out of a prewar population of 250,000 survived and many were killed by the people they had lived among.

The death camps also dealt with homosexuals (of whom tens of thousands are estimated to have perished) and Roma people. Figures are difficult to ascertain for the Roma, partly because many died in the puppet state of Croatia where records were barely kept. However, at least 250,000 Roma are thought to have died. Other groups—Freemasons, Jehovah's Witnesses, or any political opponents of the Nazis—were also killed in the camps.

Additionally, the Nazis treated Slavs as *Untermensch* (subhuman) and were happy for them to die by whatever means. In Poland, for example, about two million non-Jews died in the war, probably 200,000 in concentration camps and the remainder through starvation or targeted killings such as in the aftermath of the Warsaw Uprising. This racist attitude was applied particularly to Red Army prisoners, over two million of whom died from starvation or poor treatment.

Above: Jews disembark from a train at a camp. The dedicated death camps, such as Treblinka (where up to one million people may have died) were quite small and simple. Treblinka was run by 50 German and 150 Ukrainian guards, plus 1,000 Jewish prisoners. The Jews would arrive in trains, be separated into groups, and forced to strip and hand over any valuables. Women had their heads shaved (the hair was used to stuff mattresses). The naked victims were then marched to a "shower block," the doors bolted, and the gas turned on. The corpses were then dragged out and thrown into a mass grave or burned in special ovens.

Above: Electrified fences, guard towers, and searchlights at Strutthof Concentration Camp near Danzig.

Above: "Children of tender age were invariably exterminated, since by reason of their youth they were unable to work," Auschwitz commandant Rudolf Hoess explained after the war to his interrogators.

Above: A camp gas chamber. Many chambers were labeled "shower block

Right: Some of the 13,000 unbu dead that the British Army found u it liberated Belsen. Belsen becam concentration camp in 1942. It ha gas ovens, but an estimated 50, inmates died there, including A Frank, who died of typ

Left: Female guards at Belsen concentration camp, a photograph taken after the British Army had liberated the camp. Front center is Irma Grese, known to inmates as the "Beast of Belsen," and mistress of camp commandant Josef Kramer.

Above: The ovens at Belsen concentration camp. Disposing of the mass of bodies was a big problem for camp authorities, and mass graves were soon filled. The ovens were the answer. The camp authorities even raked over the ashes of the dead to find anything of value that had been missed previously, whether gold teeth or hidden personal effects such as rings.

death camp was located at Auschwitz in Upper East Silesia. Originally opened as a camp for mostly Polish political prisoners, it was rapidly expanded as a work camp and then as a site for extermination. The camp itself was divided into three parts: Auschwitz 1 was the original camp; Auschwitz 2 at Birkenau, built to accommodate 200,000 victims, was the death camp; and Auschwitz 3, the industrial center. It is estimated that around two million Jews were murdered at the Auschwitz complex alone.

The death camps

The SS had estimated the need to exterminate 11 million Jews, and so other death camps were set up to deal with the numbers being sent for annihilation. In early 1942, therefore, four were established in Poland: Belzec, Lublin, Sobibor, and Treblinka, with two others being established in "Greater Germany": Chelmno and Auschwitz. Belzec had a killing capacity of 15,000 a day, while Treblinka and Lublin could kill 25,000 a day. There were other concentration camps, and although they were not death camps, atrocities and murders took place in all of them over a long period of time, and the conditions for inmates were horrendous. Their names have since become associated with all the evils of Nazism: Dachau, Sachsenhausen, Buchenwald, Ravensbrück, Mauthausen, Bergen-Belsen, Theresienstadt, Flossenbürg, and Natzweiler.

Six million Jews died at the hands of the Nazis during World War II. Rudolf Würster, a young Luftwaffe recruit, provides a suitable conclusion. He witnessed the murder of Jews in Poland but kept the information to himself, and "confided only to my closest friends my feelings that we were going to have a lot to answer for if we lost the war."

1939

SEPTEMBER 1
POLAND
A German force of 53 divisions, supported by 1,600 aircraft, crosses the German and Slovak borders into Poland in a pincer movement. World War II has begun.

SEPTEMBER 3
BRITAIN AND FRANCE
Britain and France declare war on Nazi Germany after the Nazis ignore their demands to immediately withdraw from Poland.

SEPTEMBER 9
POLAND
A Polish counterattack is launched over the Bzura River against Germany's Eighth Army. It only achieves short-term success. The Polish Army is rapidly falling to pieces under the relentless German attacks.

SEPTEMBER 17–30
POLAND
In accordance with a secret pact with Germany, the Soviet Red Army invades Poland. Little resistance is encountered on Poland's eastern border as the Polish Army is fighting for its life to the west.

SEPTEMBER 18–30
POLAND
Poland is defeated and split into two zones of occupation divided by the Bug River. Germany has lost 10,572 troops and the Soviet Union has 734 men killed in the campaign. Around 50,000 Poles are killed and 750,000 captured.

SEPTEMBER 29
SOVIET UNION
After occupying Poland, the Soviet Union concentrates on extending its control over the Baltic Sea region. During the next few weeks it gains bases and signs "mutual assistance" agreements with Lithuania, Latvia, and Estonia. Finland, however, will not

agree to the Soviet Union's demands and prepares to fight.

OCTOBER 14
SEA WAR, NORTH SEA
The British battleship *Royal Oak* is sunk, with 786 lives lost, after *U-47* passes through antisubmarine defenses at Scapa Flow in the Orkneys.

NOVEMBER 30
EASTERN FRONT, FINLAND
A Soviet army of over 600,000 men, backed by air and naval power, attacks Finland. Highly-motivated Finnish troops use their familiarity with the terrain and use their ability to ski through snow-covered areas to launch hit-and-run raids on Red Army units bogged down in the snow.

DECEMBER 16
FINLAND
The Red Army begins a major new offensive. To compensate for their lack of armor and artillery, the Finns use improvised explosive devices ("Molotov Cocktails," named after the Soviet foreign minister) to destroy enemy tanks.

DECEMBER 13
ATLANTIC OCEAN
British ships fight the German pocket battleship *Graf Spee* at Battle of the River Plate. The *Graf Spee* is scuttled by its crew on the 17th.

1940

MARCH 11
FINLAND
The Treaty of Moscow between Finland and the Soviet Union is signed, ending the Winter War. Finland retains its independence but has to surrender the Karelian Isthmus and Hangö – 10 percent of its territory. Campaign losses: 200,000 Soviet troops and 25,000 Finns.

APRIL 9
NORWAY/DENMARK
A German invasion force, including surface ships, U-boats, and 1,000 aircraft, attacks Denmark and Norway. Denmark is overrun immediately.

APRIL 14–19
NORWAY
An Allied expeditionary force of over 10,000 British, French, and Polish troops lands in Norway.

MAY 7–10
BRITAIN
Prime Minister Neville Chamberlain is severely criticized over the Norwegian campaign. He resigns and is replaced by Winston Churchill.

MAY 10
THE LOW COUNTRIES
German forces invade the Low Countries. But the main German attack will take place in the south, in the Ardennes region of France.

MAY 12–14
FRANCE
German forces reach the Meuse River and fight their way across at Sedan and Dinant on the 13th. German armor advances westward rapidly, opening a 50-mile (75-km) gap in the Allied line. Allied units retreat to the Channel port of Dunkirk.

MAY 26
FRANCE/BELGIUM
Operation Dynamo, the evacuation of Allied forces from the Dunkirk area, begins using small boats and naval vessels.

MAY 31
UNITED STATES
President Franklin D. Roosevelt launches a "billion-dollar defense program" to bolster the armed forces.

JUNE 1–9
NORWAY
After Britain and France reveal to the

Norwegians that they are to begin an evacuation, troops begin to withdraw. King Haakon orders his Norwegians to stop fighting on June 9.

June 3–4

FRANCE

Operation Dynamo ends. The remarkable operation has rescued 338,226 men—two-thirds of them British—from the Dunkirk beaches.

June 16–24

FRANCE

Marshal Henri-Philippe Pétain, the new French president, requests an armistice on the 17th. It is signed on the 22nd. Germany occupies two-thirds of France, including the Channel and Atlantic coastlines.

July 1

ATLANTIC OCEAN

The "Happy Time" begins for U-boat crews as their range is increased now that they have bases in French ports. This lasts until October. U-boat crews inflict serious losses on Allied convoys.

July 10

BRITAIN

The Battle of Britain begins. Hermann Göring, the Nazi air force chief, orders attacks on shipping and ports in the English Channel.

July 21

SOVIET UNION

The Soviets annex Lithuania, Latvia, and Estonia.

August 24–25

BRITAIN

The Luftwaffe inflicts serious losses on the Royal Air Force (RAF) during attacks on its main air bases in southeast England, straining the resources of Fighter Command to the breaking point in a few days.

August 26–29

GERMANY

The RAF launches a night raid with 81 aircraft on Berlin following a similar raid on London. Hitler is outraged and vows revenge. German aircraft are redirected to make retaliatory raids on London. This relieves the pressure on Fighter Command's air bases.

September 7–30

AIR WAR, BRITAIN

Full-scale bombing raids on London— the "Blitz"—begin with 500 bombers and 600 fighters.

October 28

GREECE

Italy attacks Greece from Albania. The winter weather limits air support and thousands die of cold.

November 5

UNITED STATES

President Franklin D. Roosevelt is elected for a third term.

November 11–12

MEDITERRANEAN

At the Battle of Taranto, British torpedo aircraft from the carrier *Illustrious* destroy three Italian battleships and damage two other vessels during the raid on the Italian base.

December 9–11

EGYPT

The British launch their first offensive in the Western Desert. The Western Desert Force (31,000) attacks the fortified camps that have been established by the Italians in Egypt. Some 34,000 Italians are taken prisoner as they retreat rapidly from Egypt.

1941

January 2

POLITICS, UNITED STATES

President Franklin D. Roosevelt announces a program to produce 200 freighters—"Liberty" ships—to support the Allied Atlantic convoys.

February 14

NORTH AFRICA

To aid the faltering Italians, the first units of General Erwin Rommel's Afrika Korps land at Tripoli.

March 11

UNITED STATES

President Franklin D. Roosevelt signs the Lend-Lease Act that allows Britain to obtain supplies without having to immediately pay for them in cash.

April 6–15

YUGOSLAVIA / GREECE

Thirty-three German divisions, with

Italian and Hungarian support, invade Yugoslavia from the north, east, and southeast. German forces also attack Greece from the north.

April 17

YUGOSLAVIA

Yugoslavia surrenders to Germany. Immediately, guerrilla forces emerge to resist the Nazi occupation.

April 27

GREECE

German forces occupy Athens. Campaign dead: Greek 15,700; Italian 13,755; German 1,518; and British 900.

May 20–22

CRETE

A German force of 23,000 men, supported by 600 aircraft, attacks Crete. The Germans launch the first major airborne operation in history.

May 23–27

ATLANTIC OCEAN

British ships find the German battleship *Bismarck* and cruiser *Prinz Eugen* in the Denmark Straits between Iceland and Greenland. The *Bismarck* sinks the cruiser *Hood* and damages the battleship *Prince of Wales*, but is then sunk.

May 28–31

CRETE

Crete falls to the Germans. British losses are 1,742 men, plus 2,011 dead and wounded at sea, while Germany has 3,985 men killed.

June 22

SOVIET UNION

Germany launches Operation Barbarossa, the invasion of the Soviet Union, with three million men divided into three army groups along a 2000-mile (3200-km) front. Army Group North strikes toward the Baltic and Leningrad. Army Group Center aims to take Smolensk and then Moscow. Army Group South advances toward the Ukraine and the Caucasus.

July 31

GERMANY

Reinhard Heydrich, Germany's security chief and head of the SS secret police, receives orders to begin creating a draft plan for the murder of the Jews, which becomes known as the "Final Solution."

SEPTEMBER 30
SOVIET UNION
Operation Typhoon, the German attack on Moscow, officially begins.

NOVEMBER 26
PACIFIC OCEAN
The Japanese First Air Fleet leaves the Kurile Islands on a mission to destroy the U.S. Pacific Fleet at Pearl Harbor, Hawaii.

DECEMBER 7
HAWAII
The Japanese attack Pearl Harbor. Over 183 Japanese aircraft destroy six battleships and 188 aircraft, damage or sink 10 other vessels, and kill 2,000 servicemen. The Japanese lose 29 aircraft.

DECEMBER 8
SOVIET UNION
Adolf Hitler reluctantly agrees to suspend the advance on Moscow for the duration of the winter.

DECEMBER 11
AXIS
Germany and Italy declare war on the United States.

1942

JANUARY 10–11
DUTCH EAST INDIES
A Japanese force begins attacking the Dutch East Indies to secure the oil assets of this island chain.

JANUARY 20
GERMANY
At the Wannsee Conference, Berlin, deputy head of the SS Reinhard Heydrich reveals his plans for the "Final Solution" to the so-called "Jewish problem." Heydrich receives permission to begin deporting all Jews in German-controlled areas to Eastern Europe to face either forced labor or extermination.

FEBRUARY 8–14
SINGAPORE
Japanese troops capture Singapore. Japan has fewer than 10,000 casualties in Malaya. British forces have lost 138,000 men.

APRIL 9
PHILIPPINES
Major General Jonathan Wainright, commanding the U.S. and Filipino forces, surrenders to the Japanese.

APRIL 18
JAPAN
Lieutenant Colonel James Doolittle leads 16 B-25 bombers, launched from the carrier *Hornet*, against targets in Japan, including Tokyo.

JUNE 4
PACIFIC OCEAN
The Battle of Midway begins. Japan's Admiral Chuichi Nagumo aims to seize the U.S. base at Midway and then destroy the U.S. Pacific Fleet. Japan deploys 165 vessels, including eight carriers. The U.S. Navy has a smaller force but has three carriers. The loss of half of its carrier strength in the battle, plus 275 aircraft, puts Japan on the defensive in the Pacific.

JUNE 21
LIBYA
Following the Allied withdrawal into Egypt, the Tobruk garrison falls following German land and air attacks.

JUNE 28
SOVIET UNION
Germany launches its summer offensive, Operation Blue, with its Army Group South attacking east from Kursk toward Voronezh.

JULY 4–10
SOVIET UNION
The siege of Sevastopol ends with the Germans capturing 90,000 men.

AUGUST 7–21
GUADALCANAL
The U.S. 1st Marine Division lands on Guadalcanal Island to overwhelm the Japanese garrison.

SEPTEMBER 2
POLAND
The Nazis are "clearing" the Jewish Warsaw Ghetto. Over 50,000 Jews have been killed by poison gas or sent to concentration camps.

OCTOBER 23
EGYPT
The Battle of El Alamein begins. An attack by 195,000 Allied troops against

104,000 Axis men begins.

NOVEMBER 2–24
EGYPT / LIBYA
Rommel, severely lacking supplies, decides to withdraw from El Alamein. Germany and Italy have had 59,000 men killed, wounded, or captured. The Allies have suffered 13,000 killed, wounded, or missing.

NOVEMBER 19
SOVIET UNION
General Zhukov launches a Soviet counteroffensive at Stalingrad to trap the Germans in a massive pincer movement.

1943

FEBRUARY 2
SOVIET UNION
The siege of Stalingrad ends. Field Marshal Friedrich Paulus and 93,000 German troops surrender.

FEBRUARY 14–22
TUNISIA
In the Battle of Kasserine Pass, Rommel's forces cause panic among U.S. troops. He loses 2,000 men; the Americans 10,000.

APRIL 17
GERMANY
The U.S. Eighth Army Air Force attacks Bremen's aircraft factories from its bases in eastern England. Sixteen of the 115 B-17 Flying Fortress bombers from the raid are lost.

MAY 13
TUNISIA
Axis forces surrender. Some 620,000 casualties and prisoners have been sustained by Germany and Italy. Allied campaign losses: French 20,000; British 19,000; and Americans 18,500.

JULY 5
SOVIET UNION
Over 6,000 German and Soviet tanks and assault guns take part in the Battle of Kursk.

JULY 9
SICILY
U.S. and British troops begin the attack on Sicily.

JULY 12–13
SOVIET UNION
At Kursk, the Soviets launch a counteroffensive around Prokhorovka and an enormous tank battle develops. The German offensive is defeated.

AUGUST 11–17
SICILY
The Germans finally start withdrawing before U.S. forces enter Messina on the 17th.

SEPTEMBER 9
ITALY
Lieutenant General Mark Clark's U.S. Fifth Army, plus the British X Corps, lands in the Gulf of Salerno.

SEPTEMBER 25
SOVIET UNION
The Soviets recapture Smolensk in their continuing offensive. Germany's Army Group Center is now falling back in some disarray.

NOVEMBER 6
SOVIET UNION
The Soviets recapture Kiev.

DECEMBER 26
ARCTIC OCEAN
At the Battle of the North Cape, the German battleship *Scharnhorst* is sunk.

1944

JANUARY 14–27
SOVIET UNION
The Red Army ends the German blockade of Leningrad. Some 830,000 civilians have died during the siege.

JANUARY 22
ITALY
Troops of the Allied VI Corps make an amphibious landing at Anzio, behind the German lines.

MARCH 7–8
BURMA / INDIA
Operation U-Go, the Japanese offensive to drive the Allies back into India by destroying their bases at Imphal and Kohima, begins.

MARCH 20–22
ITALY
Despite further frontal attacks by New Zealand troops, the German defenders repulse all efforts to dislodge them from Monte Cassino.

MAY 18
ITALY
The Allies capture the monastery of Monte Cassino.

JUNE 6
FRANCE
The Allies launch the greatest amphibious operation in military history—D-Day. Some 50,000 men land on five invasion beaches to establish a toehold in Normandy. Allied casualties are 2,500 dead.

JUNE 19–21
PHILIPPINE SEA
Battle of the Philippine Sea. Japan's Combined Fleet is defeated by the U.S. Fifth Fleet. The Japanese lose 346 aircraft and two carriers. U.S. losses are 30 aircraft and slight damage to a battleship.

JUNE 22
SOVIET UNION
The Red Army launches Operation Bagration against Germany's Army Group Center.

JULY 20
GERMANY
An attempt is made by German officers to assassinate Adolf Hitler. It fails to kill the Führer.

AUGUST 1
POLAND
The Warsaw uprising begins. Some 38,000 soldiers of the Polish Home Army battle with about the same number of German troops.

AUGUST 25
FRANCE
The commander of the German garrison of Paris, General Dietrich von Choltitz, surrenders to the Allies.

SEPTEMBER 17
HOLLAND
Operation Market Garden, an Allied armored and airborne thrust across Holland to outflank the German defenses, begins. Paratroopers land at Arnhem, Eindhoven, and Nijmegen to capture vital bridges.

SEPTEMBER 22–25
HOLLAND
The paratroopers fall back from Arnhem, leaving 2,500 dead behind.

OCTOBER 2
POLAND
The last Poles in Warsaw surrender as the Germans crush the uprising. Polish deaths number 150,000. The Germans have lost 26,000 men.

OCTOBER 20
PHILIPPINES
As the U.S. Sixth Army lands on Leyte Island, General Douglas MacArthur wades ashore and keeps a promise he made two years earlier: "I shall return."

OCTOBER 23–26
PHILIPPINES
Following the U.S. landings on Leyte, the Japanese Combined Fleet is defeated at the Battle of Leyte Gulf.

DECEMBER 16–22
BELGIUM
Hitler launches Operation Watch on the Rhine, his attempt to capture Antwerp. The thick fog means the Germans achieve complete surprise. But they fail to capture Bastogne.

1945

JANUARY 9
PHILIPPINES
The U.S. Sixth Army makes unopposed amphibious landings on Luzon.

JANUARY 27
POLAND
The Red Army liberates the Nazi death camp at Auschwitz.

JANUARY 28
BELGIUM
The last bits of the German "bulge" in the Ardennes are wiped out. The Germans have had 100,000 killed, wounded, and captured in their defeat. The Americans have had 81,000 killed, wounded, or captured, and the British 1,400 killed.

JANUARY 30
GERMANY
The Red Army is only 100 miles (160 km) from Berlin.

FEBRUARY 4–11

SOVIET UNION

Marshal Joseph Stalin, President Franklin D. Roosevelt, and Prime Minister Winston Churchill meet at the Yalta Conference in the Crimea to discuss postwar Europe. The "Big Three" decide that Germany will be divided into four zones, administered by Britain, France, the United States, and the Soviet Union.

FEBRUARY 13–14

GERMANY

The RAF mounts a night raid on Dresden. The 805 bombers inflict massive damage on the city, killing 50,000 people.

FEBRUARY 17

IWO JIMA

Under the command of Lieutenant General Holland M. Smith, the U.S. Marines land on the island of Iwo Jima. The attackers are hit by intense artillery and small-arms fire from the 21,000-man Japanese garrison.

MARCH 16

IWO JIMA

The island of Iwo Jima is declared secure by the Americans. They have lost 6,821 soldiers and sailors, while of the 21,000-man Japanese garrison, only 1,083 are taken prisoner.

MARCH 22–31

GERMANY

The Allied crossings of the Rhine River begin. German resistance is negligible.

APRIL 1

OKINAWA

Operation Iceberg, the U.S. invasion of the island, commences. The island, only 325 miles (520 km) from Japan, is an excellent springboard for the proposed invasion of the Japanese mainland.

APRIL 7

PACIFIC OCEAN

The Japanese *Yamato*, the world's largest battleship, is sunk at sea during an attack by U.S. warplanes.

APRIL 9

ITALY

The final campaign in Italy begins as the U.S. Fifth and British Eighth Armies attack the Germans.

APRIL 12

UNITED STATES

President Franklin D. Roosevelt dies of a cerebral hemorrhage. Vice President Harry S. Truman takes over the position of president.

APRIL 16

GERMANY

The Soviet offensive to capture Berlin commences with a total of 2.5 million men, 41,600 guns and mortars, 6,250 tanks and self-propelled guns, and 7,500 combat aircraft. The Germans have one million men, 10,400 guns and mortars, 1,500 tanks or assault guns, and 3,300 combat aircraft.

APRIL 27

GERMANY

"Fortress Berlin" has been reduced to an east-to-west belt 10 miles (16 km) long by three miles (5 km) wide. German forces within the city are affected by widespread desertions and suicides.

APRIL 28

ITALY

Former Italian dictator Benito Mussolini and his mistress Claretta Petacci are captured by partisans. They are both shot.

APRIL 30

GERMANY

Adolf Hitler and Eva Braun commit suicide in the Führerbunker in Berlin.

MAY 2

GERMANY

Following a savage three-day battle, in which half the garrison has been killed, Berlin, the capital of Nazi Germany, falls to the Red Army.

MAY 3

BURMA

Following 38 months of Japanese occupation, Rangoon falls to the Allies without a fight.

JUNE 22

OKINAWA

All Japanese resistance on the island ends. The Japanese have lost 110,000 during the fighting. The U.S. Tenth Army has suffered 7,613 men killed or missing, and 31,807 wounded.

JULY 17–AUGUST 2

GERMANY

The Potsdam Conference takes place in Berlin. The "Big Three"—U.S. President Harry Truman, Soviet Marshal Joseph Stalin, and British Prime Minister Clement Attlee (who had defeated Churchill in a general election on July 5)—meet to discuss postwar policy. Japan is informed that an immediate surrender would result in the continued existence of its nation, but further resistance will lead to the "utter devastation of the Japanese homeland." This is a veiled reference to the use of atomic weapons against Japan itself.

AUGUST 6

JAPAN

The B-29 Superfortress *Enola Gay* drops an atomic bomb on the Japanese city of Hiroshima, killing 70,000 people and wounding 100,000.

AUGUST 9

MANCHURIA

A massive Soviet offensive by 1.5 million men begins against the Japanese Kwantung Army.

AUGUST 9

JAPAN

A second U.S. atomic bomb is dropped on Nagasaki. It kills 35,000 people and injures a further 60,000.

AUGUST 10

JAPAN

Following a conference, during which the emperor voices his support for an immediate acceptance of the Potsdam Proclamation, Japan announces its willingness to surrender unconditionally.

AUGUST 23

MANCHURIA

The campaign in Manchuria ends in total Soviet victory. The Japanese have had over 80,000 killed and 594,000 taken prisoner. Soviet losses are 8,000 men killed and 22,000 wounded. The Kwantung Army has been destroyed.

SEPTEMBER 2

ALLIES

Aboard the battleship *Missouri* in Tokyo Bay, Japanese officials sign the Instrument of Surrender, bringing World War II to a close.

GLOSSARY

annex To bring another country or an area of territory under the rule of the state.

Anschluss The name given to the union of Austria and Germany in 1938, when Austria became part of the Third Reich.

anti-Semitism A hatred of Jews.

appropriate To take compulsory possession of private property for the use of the state.

arson The crime of deliberately starting a destructive fire.

Aryan In German racial theory, the superior racial group to which Germans, Scandinavians, and others belonged.

assassination A murder based on political or other ideological grounds, not on personal feelings.

atrocity An act that is so atrocious that people find it horrifying.

boycott A refusal to do business with a certain group of people or an individual.

concentration camp A camp for the detention of political prisoners, refugees, and similar groups.

confiscation The seizure of private property by the state.

crematoria (singular: crematorium) Ovens for burning dead bodies.

decree An order that has the force of a law.

deportation The act of legally removing someone from a country.

dissident Someone who disagrees with a dominant political or religious system.

emigration The act of permanently leaving one's homeland to go and live in another country.

euthanasia The practice of killing those who are helpless or sick.

extermination To get rid of a group such as an entire race by killing it off completely.

genetics The study of how qualities are passed on from parents to their children.

genocide The systematic destruction of a racial, political, or cultural group.

persecution The harrassment or punishment of a group of people who have different beliefs or who come from a different racial, cultural, or religious background.

petition To make a formal request about something, often in writing.

pogrom An organized massacre of defenseless people, usually Jews.

propaganda The use of biased or inaccurate information to persuade people to believe a particular viewpoint or to reject another.

putsch A German word for uprising.

storm trooper A member of the Nazi SA or SS, with a reputation for aggression and brutality.

torture The deliberate infliction of great pain on an individual, either as a punishment or in order to get information.

troops Groups of soldiers.

FURTHER READING

»»»» BOOKS

Altman, Linda Jacobs. *Hidden Teens, Hidden Lives* (The Holocaust in Primary Sources). Enslow Publishers Inc., 2010.

Boyne, John. *The Boy in the Striped Pajamas*. David Fickling Books, 2006.

Byers, Anne. *Rescuing the Danish Jews: A Heroic Story from the Holocaust* (The Holocaust Through Primary Sources). Enslow Publishers Inc., 2011.

Colbert, David. *Anne Frank* (10 Days). Aladdin, 2008.

Deem, James M. *Auschwitz: Voices from the Death Camp* (The Holocaust Through Primary Sources). Enslow Publishers Inc., 2011.

Downing, David. *The Nazi Death Camps* (World Almanac Library of the Holocaust). Gareth Stevens Publishing, 2005.

Gitlin, Martin. *The Holocaust* (Essential Events). ABDO Publishing Company, 2010.

Mara, Wil. *Kristallnacht: Nazi Persecution of the Jews in Europe* (Perspectives On). Benchmark Books, 2009.

Norton, James R. *The Holocaust: Jews, Germany, and the National Socialists* (Genocide in Modern Times). Rosen Publishing Group, 2008.

Streissguth, Thomas. *Adolf Eichmann: Executing the "Final Solution"* (Holocaust Heroes and Nazi Criminals). Enslow Publishers Inc., 2005.

Thomson, Ruth. *Terezin: Voices from the Holocaust*. Candlewick Press, 2011.

Trszynska-Frederick, Luba, and Michelle Roehm McCann. *Luba: The Angel of Bergen–Belsen*. Tricycle Press, 2003.

Wood, Angela Gluck. *Holocaust: The Events and their Impact on Real People*. DK Children, 2007.

Zullo, Allan. *Escape: Children of the Holocaust*. Scholastic Paperbacks, 2011.

»»»» WEB SITES

Due to the changing nature of Internet links, Rosen Publishing has developed an online list of Web sites related to the subject of this book. This site is updated regularly. Please use this link to access the list:

http://www.rosenlinks.com/WW2/Holo

INDEX

INDEX